THE GREAT BOOK
OF 1990's TRIVIA

Crezy Random Facts
& 90s Trivia

TRIVIA BILL'S NOSTALGIC
TRIVIA BOOKS VOL.2

BY
Bill O'Neill

DON'T FORGET YOUR
FREE BOOKS

**GET THEM FOR FREE ON
WWW.TRIVIABILL.COM**

CONTENTS

INTRODUCTION

Issues of civil rights, war, reform, political scandal, environmentalism, and technology, which structured the 20th Century, provided a frame for the 1990s. The last decade of the century began with the dismantling of the Soviet Union, the devolution of communism, and the end of a long arduous Cold War between powerful nations.

Many thought that the events that closed the 1980s and started the 1990s would bring international peace, but political ideology moved from a cold war to hot ethnic and religious battles that were far bloodier.

Without two superpowers, the United States and the U.S.S.R., to hold together the world through applied force, numerous ethnic groups fought diligently with their neighbors and internally for their independence, and some attempted the even harder task of securing lands they had once claimed. A multitude of the states of the former Soviet Union engaged in many of these disputes, but no place was as troubled and divided as Yugoslavia, which was riddled with issues involving culture, ethnicity, and religion.

As situations around the world boiled, a new world economy formed that had no borders and those who played the international card over nationalistic ideas saw prosperity, especially as the threat of nuclear war dissipated. However, the United States played isolationist when it came to many of the conflicts, as the politicians in power were reluctant to involve themselves with world affairs unless it involved trade. After the wall fell in Berlin, the U.S. was more inclined to focus on domestic affairs rather than issues abroad.

Sometimes domestic affairs forced the issue, as when political scandal at the White House had consumed the U.S. under President Bill Clinton, which culminated in a presidential impeachment, or when the economy reached new heights in growth and unemployment declined. The civil rights movement continued its evolution as women and minorities gained so much ground that the U.S. Supreme Court and many institutions questioned the wisdom of affirmative action policies. Gay and lesbian rights also moved to the forefront of the equal rights movement as the result of a decision by the Clinton White House to open up the military to homosexuals through a "Don't Ask, Don't Tell" policy that missed the mark.

In the end, a series of natural disasters such as hurricanes, earthquakes, and floods, as well as school shootings and acts of terrorism, which spared no region, led to a galvanized nation and new initiatives to thwart violence, gain environmental control, and prepare for emergencies of any kind.

CHAPTER ONE
1990

MAJOR EVENTS

End of the Cold War

Political revolutions are rare, and they never just "happen." They are usually part of numerous processes that come into fruition well before they are recognizable by historians and political experts. Cold War ideology and competition among militaries began in World War II's aftermath.

At the end of the war, the Soviet Union drove the Nazis out of their territory and back into Germany. At the conclusion of the war, the Soviets established friendly governments in every Eastern European nation occupied by its forces. They also infiltrated other governments, which formed a Soviet empire that stretched from western Germany and east across Europe and Asia.

Communist revolutions in both China in 1948 and Cuba in 1959 added to their growing empire; at least, that is how the West perceived it. From 1945 to 1990, the ideological competition for worldwide allies between the United States and the U.S.S.R. was constant. The two dominating superpowers took pleasure in any activity they designed to destabilize regimes friendly to their Cold War enemy.

In addition, they both maintained a military rivalry to the point of overkill, maintaining large and complex caches of nuclear weapons, which they called nuclear deterrence. This competition led to the destruction of the Soviet Union because the United States stayed strong in the technological fields and that strength resulted in powerful growth and wealth, while the Soviet Union, almost exclusively, spread its resources across numerous occupied territories and its stockpile of weapons, which stagnated and destroyed their economy.

In 1985 Mikhail Gorbachev became the leader of the Soviet Union, and he readily recognized the growing divide between the Soviet decay and the U.S. evolution in technological abilities alone. He made the difficult suggestions to those around him that the Soviet Union could not compete with America and that the country's economy was in such a poor condition that reform was necessary.

In the late 1980s Gorbachev reduced nuclear tensions with the U.S. and sent out a message that the Eastern European states that they had once stabilized by their presence were now on their own. Citizens in those Eastern Bloc nations quickly overthrew their leaders and the Berlin Wall opened on November 9, 1989. By January 1, 1990, every Eastern European government was in transition to independence from dictatorships built around Soviet ideology.

The Soviet Union also began to unravel as its infrastructure loosened and the Communist Party lost much of its power when Gorbachev challenged its constitution and implemented economic change by setting the old institutions on fire and moving toward democracy, free-market capitalism, and ethnic nationalism. The Soviet system disassembled as the secession of former republics began. The U.S.S.R. did not exist at the end of 1991; instead, Russia, Kazakhstan, Ukraine, Belarus, Turkmenistan, and ten additional states took its place.

Manuel Noriega Surrenders, Ending the U.S. Battle in Panama

In the midst of the collapse of the Soviet Union, President H. W. Bush made the decision to invade Panama in December 1989 in an attempt to overthrow the regime of Manuel Antonio Noriega Moreno, who had interfered in the election there, threatened U.S. citizens, and was reputedly heavily involved in drug trafficking. On January 3, 1990, after a short battle between U.S. soldiers and the Panamanian Defense Force, Noriega surrendered to American authorities and was extradited to Miami to face charges of drug smuggling, and the rightful winners of the Panamanian elections were installed in office.

Nelson Mandela is Released from a South African Prison

On February 11, 1990, Nelson Mandela, leader of the movement to end South African apartheid, was released from prison after serving 27 years. The lawyer-turned-revolutionary helped organize a paramilitary branch of the African National Congress (ANC), which is the oldest political black organization in South Africa.

The group of rebels led by Mandela engaged in guerilla warfare against the white minority government that had enacted an institutionalized system based on white supremacy and racial segregation. In 1964 he was convicted of sabotage and sentenced to life in prison. The brutal Robben Island Prison provided him with a small cell without a bed or plumbing. He was forced to do hard labor in a quarry, could write and receive one letter every six months, and receive one visitor per year for 30 minutes.

When South Africa nominated F.W. de Klerk as president in 1989, he immediately began dismantling the apartheid system. He lifted the ban on ANC activity, released Mandela, and established a multiracial government. In 1993 de Klerk and Mandela were awarded the Nobel Peace Prize, and the next year Mandela was elected South Africa's president.

Grunge Rock Dominates the Decade

Characterized by distorted instruments, melancholy lyrics, and independent voices, grunge rock emerged out of the Seattle music scene in the early 1990s. The sound was popular in Washington for most of the 1980s with hit-producing Pearl Jam and Nirvana at the head of the ship, along with Green River, Soundgarden, Blood Circus, Swallow, and TAD. As one Seattle expert, Clark Humphrey, wrote, it was an "angry, disheveled" version of rock that has "stories complete with misconceptions and more than a few downright lies."

The grunge movement represented itself as authentic street rock, and not packaged music created by major music producers. However, the popular bands among the group succeeded because they signed major record deals, leaving behind their local friends. Although, one ideology did stand upright even when major labels called upon the bands, as Humphrey stated, "There is no singular 'Seattle Sound,' but there is a common Seattle attitude. We believe in making great music and art, not in the trappings of celebrity."

The Gulf War

President H. W. Bush's first challenge after the Cold War ended was Saddam Hussein, the ruthless and unpredictable leader of Iraq who invaded Kuwait, in August 1990, and then threatened to take ownership of oilfields in Saudi Arabia. Saddam's actions had nothing to do with politics and his brazen act was emboldened by his belief that the United States would not intervene in his border dispute with Kuwait because the Bush administration was their ally, as they had been during their dispute with Iran.

However, Hussein's attack on the disputed and undefended Kuwaiti border resulted in implications that he had not considered. He had shifted the balance of power in the Middle East and when global oil supplies were threatened, the U.S. moved into action. Furthermore, President H. W. Bush, who was a fighter pilot during World War II, considered Hussein's attack on Kuwait as no different from Hitler's attack on Czechoslovakia, an act that many great nations allowed because they were unwilling to go to war for such small stakes. Bush thought that allowing Iraq's behavior to continue unimpeded would only embolden and empower them to move toward further aggression.

Bush immediately mobilized U.S. forces and demanded that Iraq withdraw from Kuwait. The U.S. President won approval from the U.S. Congress and the UN Security Council and also garnered support for his demands from allies and adversaries. In a key move, he talked Israel into remaining neutral with the understanding that Israel's participation would have allowed Saddam to evolve the conflict into a holy war against Israel, which would have made the task of the fragile coalition of Middle Eastern, American, and European allies more difficult.

The U.S.-led coalition invaded Iraq in 1991 as Operation Desert Storm began. The Iraqi resistance collapsed in overwhelming fashion as allied forces freed Kuwait. Saddam remained in power, however, and played a game of cat-and-mouse in response to the UN's demands that he permit inspections of nuclear, biological, and chemical weapons facilities and destroy any weapons of mass destruction. The war had ended, but the world had not resolved the conflict.

NEA Restrictions After Obscenity Claims

Congress established the National Endowment for the Arts (NEA) in 1965 to serve "the public good by nurturing human creativity, supporting community spirit, and fostering appreciation of the excellence and diversity of our nation's artistic accomplishments."

Over the years, it has provided grants to museums and galleries, as well as individual artists to encourage artistry in the United States by funding projects that might never have received private funding. The largely innocuous endowment made headlines in May and June 1989 when controversy erupted over NEA support for Andres Serrano whose photograph *Piss Christ* presented an image of a crucifix immersed in Serrano's urine, and Robert Mapplethorpe whose photographic images displayed acts of homoeroticism and sadomasochism.

Republican Senator Jesse Helms from North Carolina and other members of U.S. Congress criticized the NEA for funding "disgusting" and "blasphemous" art with taxpayers' money, and on June 12, 1989, the Corcoran Museum in Washington, D.C., canceled Mapplethorpe's show *The Perfect Moment* out of fear that it would lose federal funding.

Subsequently, a new NEA appropriations bill passed on October 20, 1989, and it imposed conditions on future funding. It specified that artists and institutions could not use NEA funding "to promote, disseminate, or produce materials which may be considered obscene, including but not limited to depictions of sadomasochism, homoeroticism, the sexual exploitation of children, or individuals engaged in sex acts and which, when taken as a whole, do not have serious literary, artistic, political, or scientific value." In December 1990 the bill went further to specify that if an artist used NEA grant money to create obscene images, they must return their funding.

NC-17: A New Form of Movie Regulation

In 1990 the Motion Picture Association of America replaced the "X rating" with a new "NC-17 rating" for films with excessive violence or sexuality. The new

10

rating instructed theater owners that they should not permit patrons under seventeen into these movies even if a parent accompanied them.

Since newspapers were reluctant to advertise NC-17 movies, and many theaters did not show them, directors began cutting or remaking scenes in order to earn an "R rating." *Showgirls* in 1995 became the first commercial film with an NC-17 rating, and it bombed with both critics and moviegoers.

By the mid-1990s, politicians began targeting movie violence and accused the industry of creating, at least according to Republican presidential candidate Robert Dole, "nightmares of depravity." Henry Hyde from Illinois proposed legislation that would ban the sales of violent materials to any minor, and Republican Senator John McCain of Arizona proposed a bill to require the entertainment industry to label violent products with warnings. Critics of this sort of legislation called these measures "hand-wringing," and while it might appeal to voters, it would have very little impact on the movie and music industry.

"Dr. Death" and the Right to Die

Dr. Jack Kevorkian, or "Dr. Death" as the media called him, brought the right-to-die issue to the forefront by assisting numerous terminally-ill patients with ending their lives. Most states forbade assisted suicide, and in 1990 the Supreme Court, in *Cruzan v. Direct, Missouri Department of Health*, ruled that the parents of a comatose woman with a brain injury could not remove their daughter's feeding tubes.

The Court, however, did allow the withholding of life-support measures if the person had made provisions in a "living will." In *Vacco v. Quill* in 1997, the Court ruled that terminally-ill people did not have a constitutional right to assisted suicide. Many Americans did accept these decisions, and juries have continually refused to convict Kevorkian or family members who have assisted individuals in taking their own lives when terminally ill and suffering on a daily basis.

The Development of the Internet and World Wide Web

The Internet and the World Wide Web were revolutionary technologies that created a digital culture in America during the 1990s. The "Information Superhighway" could link anyone in the world through near-instantaneous data transmissions, and terms such as "cyberspace" and "the Net" became part of common lingo.

The Internet changed mainstream-American society, the ways that companies and commerce could conduct business, and the way anyone could exchange information and interact socially.

Joseph C. R. Licklider, a psychologist at M.I.T., envisioned the notion of an Internet in August of 1962 when he wrote memos discussing his "Galactic Network" concept, which was a network of inter-connected computers. He had a vision of a global interconnection of computers, which would allow anyone with a terminal to quickly access information from other computers.

In 1962 Licklider became the first administrator of the Information Processing Techniques Office (IPTO) within the Advanced Research Projects Agency (ARPA), which was a bureau of the Department of Defense that involved computer research. The stated mission of IPTO was to "create a new generation of computational and information systems that possessed capabilities far beyond those current systems" that were available at that time. The core mission of ARPA was to ensure that the U.S. applied innovative technology to its military capabilities and prevented any technological surprises from enemies. As a result of the bureau's good research and development implementations, scientists at ARPA created the first-ever computer network in 1969 and called it the ARPANET.

The network promoted access to supercomputers among U.S. researchers through a cooperative network, and from these beginnings, the network grew to what we now call the Internet.

The creators of the Internet built it with an open-architecture, and there were no set rules as to what people could do with it. The generality of purpose and open inclusion were key aspects to the fast growth of the Internet. Since there were no controlling factions, it was easily adaptable to numerous applications, so individual connected networks could design and develop their interface in any manner to suit their specific requirements.

When the technology world boomed in the mid-1980s and the personal-computer market grew, the combination of a multitude of desktop machines and network-ready servers prompted substantial growth of the Internet. Businesses used the Internet to communicate with one another and their clients. Prodigy and CompuServe were two of the first major commercial online service providers to emerge in the mid-to-late 1980s, but by 1991 the number of Internet hosts had grown to more than 300,000.

Around that time in 1989-1990, Tim Berners-Lee, a software engineer, invented the World Wide Web while working at CERN (European Council for Nuclear Research) in Switzerland. He developed coding languages for programming computers to store information in random associations, which made it easier for people to follow threads of knowledge within the information on the Internet. Essentially, he wrote the HyperText Markup Language (HTML), a coding language that allowed users to create links in their documents and write their own web pages to connect into the World Wide Web. This led to an explosion of content and practical uses that by 1995 could be accessed by anyone with an internet connection.

The Hubble Telescope

In 1990 *Space Shuttle Discovery* carried the Hubble Space Telescope (HST) into orbit about 370 miles above Earth. Because the telescope did not observe through the distorting prism of the atmosphere, which occurred through the use of telescopes on land pointed into space, it could view objects with greater clarity, brightness, and overall detail than any telescope that existed on Earth. The telescope sent back unprecedented photos of the universe that included planets, stars, and distant galaxies that humans had never before seen. Scientists found evidence that supported the Big Bang theory and indications that the universe was younger than previously theorized, while finding young stars and an abundance of planets, signaling the greater possibility of life in outer space.

20 RANDOM FACTS FROM 1990

1. On February 7, 1990, the Soviet Union's Central Committee of the Communist Party (CCCP) voted to end its monopoly on political power.

2. On February 21, 1990, the 32nd Grammy Awards awarded *Nick of Time* by Bonnie Raitt as Album of the Year and "Wind Beneath My Wings" as Record of the Year.

3. On March 11, 1990, Lithuania declared its independence from the Soviet Union.

4. On March 15, 1990, Mikhail Gorbachev became the first executive president of the U.S.S.R.

5. On March 26, 1990, the 62nd Academy Awards awarded *Driving Miss Daisy* as Best Picture, Jessica Tandy as Best Actress for her role in the movie, and Daniel Day Lewis as Best Actor for his role in *My Left Foot*.

6. On April 1, 1990, a thousand inmates rioted in Strangeways Prison in Manchester, Britain, and almost a month into the riot, police officers stormed the facility and retook it.

7. On May 4, 1990, the North Atlantic Treaty Organization (NATO) granted full membership to Germany upon its reunification.

8. On May 4, 1990, Latvia declared itself an independent state, and Estonia followed their lead four days later.

9. On May 15, 1990, schools and hospitals in the United Kingdom banned homegrown beef because of concerns over mad-cow disease.

10. On May 20, 1990, in Romania, the National Salvation Front won a majority of the votes as Ion Iliescu was elected president in the first free election in the country since 1937.

11. On May 22, 1990, North and South Yemen merged to form the Yemen Republic.

12. On May 29, 1990, the Russian Federation elected Boris Yeltsin as its president.

13. On June 12, 1990, the Russian Federation declared itself a sovereign state.

14. On July 12, 1990, Boris Yeltsin and other reformers in the U.S.S.R. renounced their Communist Party membership.

15. On July 16, 1990, the Ukrainian Parliament voted for independent sovereignty.

16. On October 2, 1990, the German Democratic Republic ceased to exist as East and West Germany united as the Federal Republic of Germany.

17. On October 9, 1990, David Hackett Souter became an Associate Justice of the U.S. Supreme Court.

18. On November 14, 1990, pop-music group Milli Vanilli admitted to lip-synching hits such as "Girl You Know It's True," and this admission resulted in their 1989 Grammy Award for Best New Artist being stripped from them.

19. On November 23, 1990, more than 90 percent of the voters in Slovenia endorsed independence from Yugoslavia.

20. On November 27, 1990, John Major became leader of the British Conservative Party, and the next day, Margaret Thatcher resigned and Major became the Prime Minister.

TEST YOUR 1990 KNOWLEDGE
10 QUESTIONS

1) In what part of the United States did grunge rock evolve?

   a) Washington, D.C.
   b) Seattle
   c) Los Angeles

2) After Saddam Hussein invaded Kuwait, what did he threaten to do?

   a) Attack Israel
   b) Join forces with other countries in the region.

   c) Take ownership oil supplies in Saudi Arabia

3) Which Artist was involved in the controversy surrounding NEA funding?

   a) Andres Serrano
   b) Cindy Sherman
   c) Andy Warhol

4) Jack Kevorkian was called "Dr. Death" by the media for what reason?

   a) He was a convicted serial killer
   b) His patients routinely died during routine surgical procedures
   c) He assisted people with suicide

5) The Internet was created through the work of what institution?

   a) A bureau of the U.S. Department of Defense
   b) The European Organization for Nuclear Research
   c) The Stanford School of Technology

6) Where is the Hubble Telescope located?

   a) In the Arizona desert
   b) At the McDonald Observatory in Fort Davis, Texas
   c) In orbit 370 miles above Earth

7) Who did the citizens of the Russian Federation elect as their president in 1990?

   a) Mikhail Gorbachev
   b) Boris Yeltsin
   c) Vladimir Putin

8) What did the United Kingdom ban in 1990 to protect its citizens?

   a) Iraqi immigrants
   b) Beef
   c) Assault rifles

9) What musical group lost their Grammy Award after they admitted to lip-synching?

   a) Backstreet Boys
   b) Milli Vanilli
   c) Soundgarden

10) Which Supreme Court Justice was appointed in 1990?

a) Ruth Badar Ginsburg
b) Clarence Thomas
c) David Hackett Souter

ANSWERS

1) b
2) c
3) a
4) c
5) a
6) c
7) b
8) b
9) b
10) c

CHAPTER TWO
1991

MAJOR EVENTS

The Rodney King Beating

On March 3, 1991, Rodney King was driving on a California freeway when Los Angeles Police Department officers tried to stop him for speeding, but King, who had been drinking and was on parole, led the LAPD on a high-speed chase before he was forced off the road.

During King's arrest, officers used force against him, claiming that King charged at them and resisted arrest. King, on the other hand, contended that he was afraid of the officers and was trying to defend himself. Unbeknownst to anyone at the scene, a resident of a nearby apartment complex videotaped the incident. Excerpts from the tape showed a group of white police officers beating a black man who was lying on the ground, and the footage played on television news stories around the world. King became a symbol of police brutality and the divide between black and white justice grew larger.

On March 15, 1991, four of the officers involved received indictments for excessive force and unlawful assault in the beating of King, and the trial began the first week in

February 1992. The prosecution's case was straightforward, and using the 82-second videotape of the incident, they were able to effectively argue that the officers had abused their power and betrayed the public's trust. The prosecution attorneys did not make race a primary issue because the jury was composed of mostly whites.

The defense argued that King was under the influence of an illegal drug, intoxicated by alcohol, and very aggressive. The officers testified that he was erratic and aggressive because of PCP, which allowed him to withstand two stun-gun darts. The defense played the video in slow motion and analyzed it carefully, showing that each aggressive move by the police officers was in response to King's actions while resisting arrest. Neither side of the case played the accompanying audio, which contained racial slurs, which was a crucial miscalculation by the prosecution. In the end, the jury found the officers not guilty.

Rodney King filed a $15 million civil suit against the city of Los Angeles, but a civil court refused to award him anything in punitive damages.

Serial Killer Jeffrey Dahmer is Convicted and Murdered

On July 22, 1991, Jeffrey L. Dahmer was arrested for several murders in Milwaukee after police found Polaroid pictures of dismembered bodies in his apartment. Police then found several heads in his refrigerator and freezer, a photo album of dismembered victims, and a 57-gallon drum containing decomposing bodies. The serial killer was found guilty in 1992 of committing 15 of the 17 killings to which he had confessed. His insanity plea was rejected by the jury and he was sentenced to life in prison. On November 28, 1994, he was killed by a fellow prisoner.

Biosphere 2

The creators of Biosphere 2 designed it to mimic conditions on Earth (Biosphere 1) in a sealed and controlled environment for research purposes. Texas billionaire Edward P. Bass funded the project and envisioned Biosphere 2, which was located near Tucson, Arizona, as a step closer to the colonization of Mars.

The sealed environment contained five "wilderness areas," including a rain forest, desert, and an ocean. The goal of the "Biospherians" was to learn to live off the land totally isolated from the Earth's atmosphere. The eight biospherians lived within the structure from 1991 to 1993, but designers ended up disappointed by the experiment because oxygen levels inside the complex dropped very low, and nitrous oxide levels rose very high, which required emergency steps to protect the inhabitants. Defeating the purpose of the experiment, oxygen was pumped into the environment.

Furthermore, most of the animals, birds, and insects died and crop production was low, requiring the creators to provide extra food to the researchers. After the researchers evacuated the facility, Bass turned Biosphere 2 over to Columbia University to manage the space as a research project.

John Grisham Becomes the Best-Selling Author of the 1990s

The best-selling author of the 1990s John Grisham is possibly, as his agent Jay Garon stated, "the most successful author in the history of the book-publishing business." Grisham never set out to become a writer, but it found him as his desire to be an attorney faded.

Grisham was born in Jonesboro, Arkansas, and earned a law degree from the University of Mississippi. Afterwards, he built a humble practice in Southaven, Mississippi, a town of 25,000 citizens. After he spent ten years practicing personal-injury and criminal law, he had yet to experience fulfillment. "I was a street lawyer, one of a thousand in a profession that was and is terribly overcrowded," he said. "Competition was fierce; ethics often compromised; and I could never bring myself to advertise."

His transition to a best-selling author occurred unexpectedly in the De Soto County Courthouse in Hernando, Mississippi, as he listened to a twelve-year-old rape victim bravely tell her story. She inspired Grisham to spend the next three years working on his first novel *A Time to Kill*, which he published in 1989. The book told the story of a black father who takes revenge on the white men after they rape his daughter.

Numerous publishing companies rejected the book until Bill Thompson, the person who discovered Stephen King, took a chance on the novel. The publication of *A Time to Kill* did not do much to change Grisham's life. He had to continue practicing law until he published his second novel *The Firm*, which became an overnight sensation. "One day I woke up and realized that I had won the lottery," Grisham said. "I walked out of my law office without turning off the lights, and I have never looked back."

Grisham's formula for success was not traditional. He is a devout Southern Baptist, who never uses vulgar language or sex as a tool in his novels. "I have never been tempted to resort to gratuitous sex, profanity, or violence," he said. "I couldn't write a book that I would be embarrassed for my kids to read a few years from now. Plus my mother would kill me."

Furthermore, Grisham characters are not complex, though they find themselves in suspenseful situations that drive the plot of his books. "I sometimes sacrifice narrative in a deliberate effort to turn pages," he explained. "You throw an innocent person in there and get them caught up in a conspiracy and then you get them out."

By the end of 1993, *The Firm* had sold more than 12 million copies in the U.S. After *The Firm*, Grisham produced a best-seller every year: *The Pelican Brief* in 1992, *The Client* in 1993, *The Chamber* in 1994, *The Rainmaker* in 1995, *The Runaway Jury* in 1996, *The Partner* in 1997, *The Street Lawyer* in 1998, and *The Testament* in 1999. Six of his novels became motion pictures that grossed millions at the box office, and the worldwide gross income of his novels and their screen adaptations have exceeded $1 billion.

Spike Lee and His Portrait of American Race Issues

Spike Lee had two big hits in the 1980s with *She's Gotta Have It* in 1986 and *Do the Right Thing* in 1989, and he made headlines in the 1990s with three thoughtful films that examine how America's citizens view race issues. *Jungle Fever*, released in 1991 starring Wesley Snipes and Annabella Sciorra, is about the consequences of a love affair between a happily-married, successful black man and his white secretary, and includes a subplot that deals with the destructive nature of the inner-city crack culture. However, Lee's biggest movie of the decade was *Malcolm X* in 1992, starring Denzel Washington and based on the 1965 book *Autobiography of Malcolm X*.

Black activists feared that Lee would give into the Hollywood establishment because Warner Brothers was producing the film, but Lee declared, "This is going to be my vision of Malcolm X," and in the end, the film offered a balanced and intellectual take on the black separatist leader. It included his speeches on race separatism, infighting among black nationalists, and his transcendent experience in Mecca.

Another Lee movie *Get on the Bus* was released in 1996 and followed a group of 20 black men who took a cross-country bus trip to attend the 1995 Million Man March in Washington D.C. The movie does not stray from the anti-Semitism and white racism of Louis Farrakhan, who organized the march, but does present the Million Man March as a movement about family and mutual understanding instead of focusing on Farrakhan and his racist views.

Nirvana and the Death of Kurt Cobain

The most well known of the grunge bands was Nirvana, which was formed in 1986 in Olympia, Washington, by Kurt Cobain and Krist Novoselic. In 1988 the group and drummer Dave Grohl signed a record deal with Sub Pop Records and released the single "Love Buzz."

Everett True, a writer for the *British New Musical Express*, reviewed the band and its Seattle area cohorts, creating interest in the grunge movement, particularly Nirvana, which smashed musical equipment and used sound-system feedback and musical distortion to accompany their emotive lyrics. The band's first album *Bleach*, which released in June 1989, was unpolished, though Cobain demonstrated his melodic ability and lyrical creativity through the violent instrumentation that accompanied the lyrics.

In 1991 Nirvana parted ways with Sub Pop and signed with David Geffen's DGC Records before recording their second album *Nevermind*. By October the album had gone gold, and today, *Spin* magazine lists the album as the top recording in the 1990s. According to writer Clark Humphrey, *Nevermind* "was a bracing jolt of post-adolescent energy and attitude that managed to unite metalheads and alternative music types alike, while roping in those curious listeners attracted by the subversive single 'Smells Like Teen Spirit.'" Thereafter, the band performed on *Saturday Night Live* and recorded an acoustic session for *MTV Unplugged*. In 1993 they released *In Utero*.

Despite their success, a heroin addiction consumed Kurt Cobain, and he nearly overdosed on a sedative in Rome in 1994 before killing himself with a shotgun later in the same year. His death ended Nirvana as well because the band members dissolved the group and moved on to other musical projects. Cobain left behind a daughter and Courtney Love, who had been his wife since 1992.

Affirmative Action and the Civil Rights Act of 1991

Since the 1970s, many governments, businesses, and universities regularly used affirmative action policies for hiring and admissions to correct the negative results of racism and gender discrimination. Beginning in the 1980s, the Supreme Court began limiting these programs and made it harder to prove employment discrimination. In an effort to bypass the position of the Justices, Congress passed the Civil Rights Act of 1991, which voided the attempts by the Court to reduce laws and policies created to address discrimination. However, the act did prohibit the use of quotas when hiring, promoting, and admitting college students.

In 1996 the Supreme Court decided not to review a ruling in *Hopwood v. Texas* that declared race-based preference admissions unconstitutional. At the time, these preferences were being used by the University of Texas Law School. This ruling set a precedent by prohibiting a different set of standards for admitting minorities. Furthermore, affirmative action programs were taking a hit at the ballot boxes in the 1990s.

California and Washington citizens approved initiatives that limited preferential hiring standards and college admissions based on race, ethnicity, color, national origin, and sex.

Justice Clarence Thomas and the Anita Hill Scandal

When Supreme Court Justice Thurgood Marshall retired in 1991, President H. W. Bush nominated Clarence Thomas, a black, conservative judge to fill the position, which created a dilemma for Senate liberals who approved of maintaining diversity on the Court, but did not like his conservative background. The Senate Judiciary Committee sent Thomas's nomination to the Senate floor, but just as the full Senate was about to vote on Thomas's nomination, accusations of sexual harassment arose.

Therefore, the committee hearings were reopened, and University of Oklahoma law professor Anita Hill testified in graphic detail about Thomas's alleged inappropriate behavior. Thomas denied the allegations and even accused the Senate of racism for even considering the issue. In a 52-48 decision, the smallest margin of approval in more than a century, the Senate confirmed Thomas.

A Decade of Change, Violence, and Dominant Players in the NFL

The 1990s was a decade of expansion and evolution for the NFL. New franchises and stadiums were born, more wild-card teams were added to the playoffs, television coverage expanded, and increased attendance and higher ratings meant more money for the league's owners and players, and higher ticket prices for fans.

Several teams moved to new cities, including the Rams from Los Angeles to St. Louis and the Oilers from Houston to Nashville, becoming the Tennessee Titans, in search of better facilities and bigger markets. The expansion teams included the Jacksonville Jaguars and the Carolina Panthers, and the league again awarded Cleveland a team and the "Browns" mascot after the city's previous franchise moved to Baltimore to become the Ravens.

Off-the-field criminal activities became the biggest concern for NFL directors and owners. The offenses ranged from possession of drugs to domestic violence, and three members of the New York Jets were arrested following a bar fight. NFL players even went to jail. The most serious offense was perpetrated by wide receiver Rae Carruth of the Carolina Panthers, who was indicted for the murder committed on November 16, 1999 during the drive-by shooting of his wife, who was pregnant with their child. Ray Lewis, a Baltimore linebacker, was also accused of murder, although the charges were dropped.

On the field, San Francisco 49ers Joe Montana began the decade as the league's MVP and won the Super Bowl in 1990. His quarterback rival Dan Marino, who led the Miami Dolphins, topped Fran Tarkenton, who played for both the Minnesota Vikings and New York Giants

(1961-1978), in four passing categories: attempts, completions, yards, and touchdowns. Jerry Rice, the 49ers wide receiver who many experts believe is the greatest NFL player in history, established all-time records for receptions and reception yardage. Dallas Cowboys running back Emmitt Smith scored 25 touchdowns in 1995, breaking the all-time record. Steve Young, who took the helm from Montana in San Francisco; Detroit running back Barry Sanders; Denver Broncos running back Terrell Davis; and the Philadelphia Eagles defender Reggie White were other high-caliber players who dominated the 1990s. In addition, the NFL was restocking itself with a talented group of players like quarterback Peyton Manning, who led the Indianapolis Colts to the playoffs in his second year, going from a 3-13 record to 13-3.

Because of these players, and in spite of the off-the-field distractions, NFL football continued to be the most popular sport in the U.S. in the 1990s, securing an eight-year broadcast deal for $17.6 billion.

Talk Radio Finds its Niche with Conservatives

Throughout the 1990s, conservative politicians, religious leaders, and other public figures bashed what they called the "liberal media," which led many of them to an underused media niche—talk radio—and they dominated the market there. On a daily basis, conservative ideologues took to the radio airwaves to attack everything from the Democratic White House and feminism to welfare and gun control.

By the mid-1990s, talk radio was the second-most popular radio format after country music in the nation, growing from 200 talk-radio stations to 1,000 by the end of the decade. A talk-radio station manager believed the conservatives dominated the format because they were more entertaining, saying that liberals "are genetically engineered not to offend anybody. People who go on the air afraid of offending are not inherently entertaining."

One thing was certain, conservative hosts in the 1990s had no issue with offending people. Rush Limbaugh, the top talk-show host of the decade, regularly targeted liberal notions, and Ken Hamblin, whose show was on more than 60 stations nationwide, targeted issues from gun control to feminism. Their impact was far-reaching, and many believed that their voice on issues influenced political choices, because the shows eventually became the primary source of news for many people.

20 RANDOM FACTS FROM 1991

1. On January 8, 1991, Pan American World Ways (Pan Am) filed for bankruptcy.

2. On January 16, 1991, U.S. warplanes attacked Iraq and occupied parts of Kuwait as Operation Desert Storm ramped up.

3. On January 17, 1991, the Dow Jones index raised 114.6 points, becoming the second-highest one-day point gain ever.

4. On January 21, 1991, CNN flexed its media missiles, dominating Gulf War coverage.

5. On February 20, 1991, the 33rd Grammy Awards awarded Album of the Year for *Back on the Block*, an album by Quincy Jones that is a compilation of songs by legendary musicians. "Another Day in Paradise" by Phil Collins was awarded Record of the Year.

6. On February 23, 1991, U.S. and UN ground troops stormed into Iraq.

7. On March 3, 1991, Iraq accepted the terms of a ceasefire after only a few weeks of battle.

8. On March 25, 1991, the 63rd Academy Awards awarded *Dances with Wolves* as Best Picture, Kathy Bates as Best Actress for her role in *Misery*, and Jeremy Irons as Best Actor for his role in *Reversal of Fortune*.

9. It was in April 1991 that the Federal Government raised the minimum wage to $4.25 per hour.

10. On April 3, 1991, the UN Security Council approved a ceasefire resolution in the Gulf War that included clearing the Iraqi government of its weapons of mass destruction.

11. On April 7, 1991, the Down Jones closed above 3,000 for the first time, as the U.S. economy bloomed.

12. On July 3, 1991, Apple Computer and IBM publicly joined forces in order to exchange technologies and develop new systems and machines.

13. Major volcanic eruptions during June and July 1991 that were experienced by communities near Philippine's Mount Pinatubo killed 722 people and left 200,000 people homeless, and these eruptions further resulted in a band of volcanic dust that temporarily cooled the climate worldwide on August 13, 1991.

14. On September 24, 1991, the Seattle grunge band Nirvana released *Nevermind*. By January 11, 1992, their "Smells Like Teen Spirit" reached number one on the Billboard single charts and became an alternative rock anthem for Generation X.

15. On October 6, 1991, NPR and *Newsday* announced Anita F. Hill's allegations of sexual harassment against Supreme Court nominee Clarence Thomas.

16. On October 20-23, 1991, a fast-spreading brush fire in the Oakland hills of California destroyed 3,000 homes and killed 24 people.

17. On October 23, 1991, Marjorie Lee Wantz and Sherry Ann Miller committed suicide in the state of Michigan with the aid of Dr. Jack Kevorkian.

18. On November 7, 1991, Earvin "Magic" Johnson Jr. announced that he had contracted the Human Immunodeficiency Virus (HIV) and retired from professional basketball.

19. On December 4, 1991, *Associated Press* reporter Terry Anderson was released after several years as a hostage in Beirut.

20. On December 21, 1991, media mogul Ted Turner married actress Jane Fonda.

TEST YOUR 1991 KNOWLEDGE
10 QUESTIONS

1) What was the biggest failure of Biosphere 2?

   a) The lack of clean drinking water for its inhabitants
   b) The lack of oxygen for its inhabitants
   c) The emotional instability of its inhabitants

2) Who was the most successful author of the 1990s?

   a) John Grisham
   b) Steven King
   c) Tom Clancy

3) Which public figure did Spike Lee direct a biography about in the 1990s?

   a) Martin Luther King
   b) Louis Farrakhan
   c) Malcolm X

4) Who did Kurt Cobain marry in the 1990s?

   a) He never married in the 1990s
   b) His longtime high school girlfriend
   c) Courtney Love

5) Which team was an expansion NFL team in the 1990s?

   a) Tennessee Titans
   b) St. Louis Rams
   c) Carolina Panthers

6) Which media format did conservative voices dominate in the 1990s?

   a) Radio
   b) Cable television
   c) Newspapers in the Midwest

7) Iraq agreed to a ceasefire in 1991, ending Operation Desert Storm. Afterward, what did the UN Security Council approve?

   a) A resolution to remove Saddam Hussein from power
   b) A resolution to limit the amount of oil Iraq could export
   c) A resolution to strip Iraq of its weapons of mass destruction

8) Which volcano unleashed massive amounts of volcanic dust in 1991 that led to a worldwide cooling of the Earth's atmosphere?

   a) Mount Vesuvius
   b) Mount Pinatubo
   c) Mount St. Helens

9) Which news source broke the news regarding sexual assault allegations against Supreme Court Justice Nominee Clarence Thomas?

   a) NPR
   b) *Newsday*
   c) All of the above

10) Which superstar announced in 1991 that they had contracted HIV, then promptly retired?

   a) Magic Johnson
   b) Greg Louganis
   c) Easy E

ANSWERS

1) b

2) a

3) c

4) c

5) c

6) a

7) c

8) b

9) c

10) a

CHAPTER THREE
1992

MAJOR EVENTS

The 1992 Albertville Winter Olympics

The end of the Soviet Union and the dismantling of the Berlin Wall played a significant role in the first Olympiad of the decade, as countries such as Lithuania, Estonia, and Latvia competed under their own flags for the first time since before World War II. Germany fielded a single team instead of two, and former Soviet athletes competed as the "Unified Team," though the flags of their separate republics were raised upon victory.

During competition, the U.S. team as a whole turned in a fair performance, placing fifth in the number of gold medals captured with five, behind Germany with 10, the Unified Team and Norway, which each had nine, and Austria with six. The showcase event medals won by the Americans were in women's figure skating, where Kristi Yamaguchi won the gold and Nancy Kerrigan won the bronze. Kerrigan's rise to figure skating prominence would become "the ice skating story" over the course of the next two years. She won the U.S. women's championship in 1993, and then was assaulted on January 6, 1994, by colleagues of rival American skater

44

Tonya Harding in an attempt to put a halt to Kerrigan's bid to go to the Olympics at Lillehammer.

The other U.S. Olympic star in Albertville was Bonnie Blair, who won two gold medals in women's speed skating: the 500 meters and 1,000 meters. No American men won gold medals in Albertville.

College Basketball Thrives

Three of the top ten highest-rated televised college basketball games were played during the decade as college hoops and "March Madness" skyrocketed in popularity, and the NCAA received a huge payday because of it, securing $6 billion for the rights to their end of the season tournament.

All the top-rated games during the decade occurred during the March Madness tournament, and included the third highest-rated game between Duke and Michigan on April 6, 1992, the fifth highest-rated game between North Carolina and Michigan on April 5, 1993, and the sixth highest-rated game between Arkansas and Duke on April 4, 1994.

Los Angeles Riots and the Beating of Reginald Denny

The end of the Rodney King trial sparked violence in Los Angeles between April 29, 1992, when a jury acquitted the police officers involved in King's beating, and May 3. South Central Los Angeles, a low-income area that is heavily populated by racial and ethnic minorities, became engulfed in conflict. Violence, looting, and general mayhem followed, resulting in 54 deaths, 2,500 injuries, and the destruction of 1,100 businesses that resulted in $1 billion in property damage. Mobs of black citizens attacked whites, Latinos, and Asians, as well other blacks that lived and worked in the area. The National Guard was eventually called in to restore order.

The chaos revealed the boiling tensions between minority races and the justice system, and the public outrage that stemmed from the original verdicts subsequently led to a federal trial in which the court found all four officers guilty.

One of the most disturbing and televised events of the riots involved the battery of a truck driver who was making his way through the area. As the news broadcast live images of the rioting, three men pulled Reginald Denny from his truck and beat him. Denny survived, and after the incident, the three men involved were identified on videotapes and eventually arrested in late 1992 for the assault of Denny, five other motorists, and two firefighters who had tried to halt the assault. All three men were found guilty.

Public reaction to the verdicts was mixed, and the press characterized the incident as "payback" for the acquittals of the police officers in the King trial and the light sentences they received in the federal trial.

The 1992 Barcelona Summer Olympics

The star of these games was Barcelona itself, a beautiful and accommodating site. Politics mattered less than in the preceding years as Cuba, North Korea, and Ethiopia ended their boycotts of the games, each nation having missed two Olympic games. South Africa, which had been absent from the Olympics since 1960, also returned. Yugoslav citizens could compete, but the nation, the Federal Republic of Yugoslavia, was banned from participating in the event because of its aggression against Croatia and Bosnia-Herzegovina and sanctions imposed by the United Nations.

American athletes again performed well, and the basketball "Dream Team" that was made up of NBA all-stars, which was the first time professionals were allowed to represent the U.S. in basketball, swept the field to a gold medal. In track and field, Carl Lewis continued to dominate as the outstanding male Summer Olympic athlete of the century, becoming one of only two individuals to win nine gold medals in track and field. He was also one of two athletes, alongside Jesse Owens, to win four gold medals in the same event. Jackie Joyner-Kersee became the outstanding female Summer Olympian of the century. During the 1992 Olympics, she won a gold medal in the heptathlon for the second consecutive Olympics and a bronze medal in the long jump. The men's swim team won six gold medals out of nineteen events, and the women's swim team won six out of twenty.

In boxing, Oscar de la Hoya was the sole U.S. victor. Three members of the freestyle wrestling team won gold medals. Jennifer Capriati won the women's singles tennis title, while Gigi and Mary Jo Fernandez won the gold in women's doubles. In all, the U.S. team won 37 gold medals, placing second only to the Unified Team in gold medal count.

Hurricane Andrew, Typhoon Iniki, and the Storm of the Century

Hurricane Andrew was the first catastrophic storm of the 1990s. The category five hurricane slammed into south Florida on August 24, 1992, with sustained winds in excess of 150 miles per hour. Homestead Air Force Base and the nearby town of Homestead were ruined by the storm as more than two million people were evacuated. Nevertheless, 26 died as a result of the storm, hundreds more were injured, and thousands lost all of their possessions.

A few weeks later, a rare Pacific typhoon, Iniki, landed on shores of the Hawaiian island of Kauai on September 11, 1992, resulting in nearly $2 billion in damage to the island. In March 1993, "the Storm of the Century" ravaged the East Coast with a late-winter storm that carried hurricane-force winds and left more than 100 people dead.

Ross Perot Changes the Face of Politics and Third Parties

Third parties and third-party candidates share a few characteristics on the American political stage. One, they are not elected. Two, they may attract voter interest in one election, but both the candidate and party disappear from the radar after the election. Three, they do not have an effective grassroots organization that carries them.

However, third-party candidate Ross Perot was different, and so was the third party he inspired and bankrolled. He ran for president as the Reform Party candidate in 1992 and 1996, and while he did lose, he had an incredible run. The Reform Party continued to exist at the end of the decade, and several well-known political figures ran as Reform candidates in the 2000 presidential election. In addition, the Reform Party had success organizing on a grassroots level, and even triumphed in the 1997 election of Jesse Ventura for governor of Minnesota. At the end of the decade, Ross Perot's political vision still continued to draw support across the United States.

The Bill Clinton Presidency

Arkansas governor Bill Clinton seemed a longshot to win the U.S. presidency in 1992. Although he was young, articulate, and energetic, he had very little national political experience. However, after winning the Democratic nomination, he was ready to take on the incumbent, President H. W. Bush, whose approval was rated high in public-opinion polls after a sound and quick victory in the Gulf War.

While Bush was strong in foreign policy, the U.S. economy had grown weak during his administration, and Clinton, a brilliant campaigner, exploited this weakness. Reading the mood of the nation, Clinton challenged Bush's domestic and economic records, knowing he had nothing to gain by focusing on foreign affairs, and his strategy worked as the United States elected Clinton with the help of third-party candidate Ross Perot, who received many votes that would have otherwise been cast for Bush.

Clinton became the first baby boomer president, and

even though he was full of fresh thoughts and adrenaline, his first term did not start well. He fulfilled his campaign promise to address healthcare reform, but Congress refused to act on his proposals. Clinton also tried to address the problems faced by homosexuals who served, or wanted to serve, in the military by instituting a "Don't Ask, Don't Tell" policy, which virtually institutionalized hypocrisy and did nothing to promote or protect gay rights.

Since Clinton was not recognized by many as "presidential" during his first year in office, and because he wasn't getting much done, Republicans dominated the midterm elections in 1994 and took control of Congress in both the Senate and the House of Representatives. To further complicate Clinton's presidency, Republican Newt Gingrich from Georgia, an aggressive and outspoken critic of the president, became Speaker of the House of Representatives, and for a time, took the policy initiative away from the White House. The turning point for Clinton occurred when Congress deadlocked on a budget, leaving the government temporarily broke, which the American public blamed the Republicans.

Clinton took action from there, and the master politician steered the ship out of harm's way by portraying himself as a moderate, and that portrayal pushed the Republicans further and further to the right, which alienated independent and moderate voters. With a healthy and soaring economy under his belt, he went into the 1996 presidential election against Republican Senator Robert Joseph Dole from Kansas, who ran a lackluster campaign against Clinton's masterful one. In November 1996, Clinton won a second term in the White House, but scandal and impeachment proceedings loomed ahead.

Director Quentin Tarantino Becomes the 1990s' Martin Scorsese

Quentin Tarantino burst onto the movie scene in 1992 with his shocking and violent movie *Reservoir Dogs*, which he wrote and directed. He also wrote and directed the biggest hit of the decade, *Pulp Fiction* in 1994, which prompted some critics to predict that Tarantino would be the "savior of American film making," and called him the new Martin Scorsese. In other words, he had the ability to depict the anxieties of the 1990s as Scorsese had done in the 1970s with his movies *Mean Streets* in 1973 and *Taxi Driver* in 1976.

Tarantino was born in Knoxville, Tennessee, but grew up in the Los Angeles suburbs. During high school, he worked at a pornographic theater, and after quitting school before graduation, he worked at Video Archives for five years, which he calls "the best video store in the Los Angeles area," and where he met Roger Avary, who worked with him on the script for *Pulp Fiction* and became a director himself.

Tarantino learned everything about directing through his addiction to movie watching, not from college courses or film school. After working on two independent movie projects in the mid-1980s, which he never completed, Tarantino treated us to *Reservoir Dogs*, and wrote the screenplay for another violent movie in 1994, Oliver

Stone's *Natural Born Killers*. *Pulp Fiction* was his next project, and Roger Ebert called the movie "a comedy about blood, guts, violence, strange sex, drugs, fixed fights, dead body disposal, leather freaks, and a wristwatch that makes a dark journey down through the generations." The movie won Tarantino and Avary an Oscar for best Original Screenplay and is a tribute to the mobster movies and pulp-fiction detective stories of the 1930s. Though his other movies of the decade, including *Jackie Brown* in 1997, drew less attention than *Pulp Fiction*, Tarantino continued to surprise and shock movie patrons with his uncanny imagination.

Women Musicians Reach New Heights

The Rolling Stone Illustrated History of Rock & Roll said in 1992 that "As more women plug in electric guitars and bash away at drum kits, they are empowered, articulating a voice that before had gone unheard. And what they have to say might just make a difference—and make it to Number One."

While Madonna's celebrity waned by the end of the 1990s, her 15-year career as "pop music chameleon," actor, and artist made her a household word and an all-time favorite icon because she was always game for controversy. MTV rejected her video for "Justify My Love" in 1990 because of nude content, and then in 1992 rejected her book *Sex*, which displayed nude pictures of her in compromising positions with members of both sexes. The book not only grossed more than $25 million the first week available in stores but also earned her negative publicity. Madonna explained, "If you read the text, it was completely tongue in cheek.

Unfortunately, my sense of humor was not something that a mainstream audience picks up. For me all it did was expose our society's hang-ups about sexuality. Yes, I took a beating, and yes, a lot of the things that were said were hurtful and unfair, but there are no mistakes. It was a great learning experience."

In 1992 she released her seventh album, *Erotica*, which sold more than two million copies, and in the same year, she signed a deal with Time Warner for $60 million. Madonna's next two albums, *Bedtime Stories* in 1994 and *Ray of Light* in 1998, also spent time at number one on the Billboard albums chart.

Another female headliner in the music business during the 1990s was Mariah Carey, who stormed onto the scene after handing a demo tape of her songs to Tommy Mottola, the president of Columbia Records, at a party. Her debut album, *Mariah Carey*, was released in 1990, and despite its simple and sweet lyrics, the album sold six million copies, while two songs reached number one. She won two Grammy Awards the following year for Best Pop Vocal Performance and Best New Artist.

Carey became a prolific singer-songwriter in the 1990s, and had more number one hits than any other female soloist with hits like "Vision of Love," "I Don't Wanna Cry," "Hero," "Dreamlover," "Fantasy," "Always Be My Baby," and "Heartbreaker."

Columbia signed Carey in response to the success of Whitney Houston, whose five-octave vocal range and melodic and smooth delivery won her international acclaim in the 1980s, which continued into the 1990s as her record sales eclipsed 100 million. Whitney Houston also starred in *The Bodyguard* along with Kevin Costner in 1992 and earned Grammys for the soundtrack album as well as the single "I Will Always Love You."

"Don't Ask, Don't Tell" and Same-Sex Marriage Debates

Most Americans were uncomfortable with the idea of extending equal rights to homosexuals, which was evident when President Clinton proposed an end to the ban on homosexuals serving in the military. After heated debate, Clinton, military leaders, and Congress reached an agreement that constituted the "Don't ask, Don't tell" policy. The new arrangement ended all questioning regarding the sexuality of those in the military while simultaneously barring soldiers from revealing their sexual preference. The gay community strongly supported Clinton in his bid for the presidency but overwhelmingly opposed what they called the "hide and lie" policy.

At the state level, homosexual rights organizations pushed for antidiscrimination legislation with limited success, though they did make up some ground. Colorado voters passed a state constitutional amendment in 1992 that nullified homosexual-rights ordinances, but the Supreme Court, in *Romer v. Evans*, ruled against the amendment in 1996. This ruling was the first time that the Supreme Court had ever applied the Fourteenth Amendment to protect against homosexual discrimination.

Furthermore, the Hawaiian Supreme Court ruled in *Baehr v. Lewin* in 1993 that a ban on homosexual marriage violated state constitutional equal rights protection. Subsequently, the victory for homosexuals in Hawaii triggered measures in more than half of the U.S. state legislatures to pass laws that banned homosexual marriages. President Clinton eventually turned this into action in 1996 when he signed Congressional legislation that denied federal recognition of same-sex marriages.

20 RANDOM FACTS FROM 1992

1. On February 1, 1992, U.S. President George H. W. Bush and Russian President Boris Yeltsin proclaimed a formal end to the Cold War.

2. On January 3, 1992, the Dow Jones closed above 3,200 for the first time, ending the day at 3201.48.

3. On January 7, 1992, President H. W. Bush arrived in Japan to talk trade, saying that he was determined to "increase access for American goods and services."

4. On January 21, 1992, in the ongoing controversy over NEA funding for controversial artists, Republican presidential hopeful Patrick Buchanan accused President H. W. Bush of supporting "filthy and blasphemous art," which caused him to fire NEA chairman John E. Frohnmayer.

5. On February 21, 1992, the United States lifted trade sanctions against China.

6. On February 24, 1992, General Motors Corporation announced a record $4.5 billion loss in 1991 and said it would close 21 plants and lay off 74,000 workers during the next four years.

7. On February 25, 1992, the 34th Grammy Awards presented Album of the Year for *Unforgettable* to Natalie Cole and awarded Record of the Year for Cole's song "Unforgettable".

8. On March 6, 1992, the computer virus "Michelangelo" struck thousands of personal computers around the world.

9. On March 30, 1992, the 64th Academy Awards awarded *The Silence of the Lambs* for Best Picture, Jody Foster as Best Actress for her role in the movie, and Anthony Hopkins as Best Actor for his role in the movie.

10. On April 23, 1992, fast-food chain McDonald's opened its first restaurant in Beijing, China.

11. During the time span of May 7-16, 1992, three *Endeavour* space shuttle astronauts simultaneously walked in space for the first time in order to retrieve and repair the Intelsat-6 satellite. The walk lasted eight hours and twenty-nine minutes.

12. On May 8, 1992, the 27th Amendment to the U.S. Constitution, which restricted compensation that members of congress had voted upon for themselves, was ratified to prevent it from going into effect until after an intervening election.

13. On June 5, 1992, the unemployment rate jumped to 7.5 percent, which was the highest level in eight years.

14. On July 2, 1992, Braniff International Airlines went out of business.

15. On June 9, 1992, the largest-ever environmental summit opened in Rio de Janeiro, Brazil. Representatives from 178 nations took part in the United Nations Conference on Environment and

Development (UNCED), otherwise known as Earth Summit. The nations discussed environmental problems on all fronts ranging from climate change to population control.

16. On June 28, 1992, two earthquakes hit southern California, including the third strongest in the United States on record for the 20th Century that registered a 7.4 on the Richter scale and killed three people.

17. On July 13, 1992, the Democratic National Convention in New York City nominated Arkansas Governor Bill Clinton for president and Senator Al Gore from Tennessee for vice president.

18. On September 11, 1992, S*pace Shuttle Endeavour* took off with a crew that included Mark C. Lee and N. Jan Davis, the first married couple in space.

19. On November 3, 1992, Clinton and Gore defeated Bush and Quail in the U.S. presidential election.

20. On December 24, 1992, President H. W. Bush pardoned all former Reagan officials who were involved in the Iran-Contra Affair.

TEST YOUR 1992 KNOWLEDGE
10 QUESTIONS

1) Which U.S. Olympic athlete won two gold medals in speed skating in 1992?

   a) Bonnie Blair
   b) Nancy Kerrigan
   c) Jackie Joyner-Kersee

2) Which of the following was the name of Ross Perot's political party?

   a) Republican
   b) Reform
   c) Green

3) In the 1992 U.S. presidential election, whom did Bill Clinton defeat?

   a) Bob Dole
   b) Newt Gingrich
   c) George H. W. Bush

4) Movie critics compared director Quentin Tarantino to what other moviemaker?

   a) Oliver Stone
   b) Martin Scorsese
   c) Francis Ford Coppola

5) Which Madonna video did MTV reject because of its sexual content?

   a) Papa Don't Preach
   b) Justify my Love
   c) Vogue

6) Which musician starred alongside Kevin Costner in the movie *The Bodyguard*?

   a) Madonna
   b) Whitney Houston
   c) Mariah Carey

7) Which fast food chain opened its first restaurant in China in 1992?

   a) Kentucky Fried Chicken
   b) McDonald's
   c) Burger King

8) What American state experienced two earthquakes in 1992?

   a) California
   b) Oregon
   c) Washington

9) In 1992, two Americans astronauts became the first to do which of the following?

   a) Get married in space
   b) Enter space as a married couple
   c) Conceive a child in space

10) On his way out of office in December 1992, President H. W. Bush did which of the following?

   a) Nominate Supreme Court Justice Clarence Thomas
   b) Propose legislation to ban same-sex marriage
   c) Pardon Reagan officials involved in the Iran-Contra Affair

ANSWERS

1) a
2) b
3) c
4) b
5) b
6) b
7) b
8) a
9) b
10) c

CHAPTER FOUR
1993

MAJOR EVENTS

The Battle at Ruby Ridge

Antigovernment militia groups were active prior to the events at Ruby Ridge, but Randy Weaver's standoff with the federal government sparked increased interest in the movement defined by the Second Amendment right to form militias and bear arms.

In February 1991, Weaver, a U.S. Army veteran and survivalist, never appeared for his trial involving felony charges for selling sawed-off shotguns to a government informant who worked for the Bureau of Alcohol, Tobacco, and Firearms (ATF). Instead, Weaver, his wife, and their two daughters, along with Kevin Harris withdrew to the family home on Ruby Ridge, near Naples, Idaho, and remained there for eighteen months.

Recognizing the potential for an armed conflict, federal agents attempted to negotiate Weaver's surrender. However, things went wrong very fast when a U.S. Marshal shot the family's dog while inspecting the woods around Weaver's cabin. Gunshots from the cabin followed, and a marshal returned fire, killing Weaver's

14-year-old son. Harris then shot one of the agents, killing him. The following day, a marshal shot and killed Weaver's wife, Vicki, as she held her infant in a doorway.

The siege at Ruby Ridge continued for eleven days until August 30, 1992, when Harris, who was wounded from a gunshot, surrendered to federal agents. Weaver and his remaining children gave up the next day.

Harris and Weaver were charged with capital murder, but a jury found both men innocent, believing that the government provoked the incident by killing Weaver's dog, his son, and then his wife. The jury also found Weaver innocent of the original charge of trafficking illegal weapons because the jury agreed with Weaver's attorney that federal officials entrapped his client.

In addition, after an extensive investigation, the U.S. Department of Justice found that federal agents overreacted and questioned the "shoot-on-sight" policy. These findings led to the Justice Department paying Weaver and his children $3.1 million for the botched incident.

The 1993 World Trade Center Bombing

On February 26, 1993, the World Trade Center in New York City was the target of a terrorist's bomb that killed six people and injured more than a thousand others. Evidence gathered by federal investigators indicated that members of several different Muslim fundamentalist groups participated in the act while pursuing a jihad, or holy war, against the American way of life.

About 50,000 people were in the 110-story complex when the 1,200-pound bomb exploded in the parking garage beneath the building. At the time, the attack, which caused $500 million in damage, was the largest act of foreign terrorism on U.S. soil.

Within 10 days after the explosion, FBI agents traced the vehicle suspected of carrying the bomb to a 26-year-old Jordanian national and a 32-year-old chemist. They, along with two other suspects, were arrested, found guilty in March 1994, and sentenced to 240 years in prison. Another suspect, Ramzi Ahmed Yousef, the 27-year-old mastermind of the attack was arrested in February 1995 in Pakistan. He was also sentenced to 240 years in prison. Other suspects are thought by federal agents to be at large.

Waco Cult Complex Burns to the Ground, Killing 76 Members

Federal law-enforcement agencies apparently failed to learn from their mistakes at Ruby Ridge. On April 19, 1993, in full view of millions of television viewers, a standoff between federal agents and a well-armed religious fringe group known as the Branch Davidians ended in a massive conflagration. Events leading up to this fiery conclusion began on February 28, 1993, when 90 heavily armed ATF agents attempted to serve a search-and-arrest warrant at the compound known as Mt. Carmel outside of Waco, Texas. Gunfire erupted and four federal agents were killed. The warrant, which was the result of almost a year of investigation and surveillance, was based on allegations that the residents possessed illegal firearms and were possibly converting semiautomatic rifles into machine guns. Later investigators found that the Davidians had stockpiled almost 400 firearms, including 48 machine guns.

During the standoff, the activities at Waco dominated national news, and Davidian leader David Koresh became a household name. After months of negotiations, the standoff was finally brought to a close when federal tanks and armored vehicles punched holes in the walls of the compound and dozens of gas canisters were fired into the building in an attempt to force the Davidians out. Following the assault, smoke poured out of the structure and within minutes, the entire compound was engulfed in flames. Seventy-six group members died, including twenty-five children under the age of fifteen. At least two dozen victims were later discovered to have died from gunshot wounds, either self-inflicted or caused by someone else in the compound. Nine Davidians escaped by fleeing the building.

Surviving Davidians were tried in federal court in 1994, having been charged with the murder of federal agents and various other crimes, including illegal weapons possession, manslaughter, and immigration violations. The Davidians argued that they had acted in self-defense against an unlawful assault conducted by the federal government. Koresh became a scapegoat for the defendants who blamed their leader, along with the government, for the incident. Defense attorneys portrayed Koresh as delusional and paranoid.

On February 26, 1994, almost one year to the day after the standoff began, the seven-week trial ended, and all of the Davidians were acquitted of the murder and conspiracy charges. Two were acquitted of all charges and freed. Seven others were convicted of lesser charges and fined or sentenced to prison terms. Over the next six years, federal investigations attempted to resolve the questions of who fired first on February 28, 1993, and how the fire started. Did the Davidians commit mass suicide or were they killed by the fire? Did federal agents, as well as Attorney General Janet Reno, act within legal bounds? As late as 1999, Congress investigated the conduct of government agencies involved in the standoff. Allegations that the Justice Department had suppressed evidence that might have incriminated federal law-enforcement agencies surfaced in the late 1990s. In the midst of court orders for government attorneys to turn over all evidence from the siege or face contempt-of-court charges, as well as constant refusals and delays in submitting documents, Congress appointed a special investigative team, led by former Republican Senator John Claggett Danforth from Missouri, to continue the probe into the standoff at Waco. While some agencies submitted subpoenaed documents, the White House refused to turn over classified documents, citing executive privilege.

In addition to the ongoing federal investigation into the conduct of law enforcement agencies, some survivors and family members of the Davidians filed a wrongful death lawsuit against the government in civil court. The case claimed that federal agents fired on sect members first and that the government was responsible for setting the fire that engulfed the compound and resulted in scores of deaths. On July 14, 2000, a jury exonerated the government in the wrongful death lawsuit; a week later Danforth's report declared that the agents were not responsible for the deaths at Waco.

The Mississippi River Flood, Northridge Earthquake, and FEMA

June-August 1993 was when the worst flood to hit the Mississippi River valley in nearly two centuries inundated farmlands and communities across nine states from North Dakota to Missouri, causing more than $10 billion in damages and taking 50 lives. An earthquake in Northridge, California, occurred in 1994, killing 61 people and injuring thousands. Hurricanes, tornadoes, floods, and wildfires continued to ravage the country over the next five years, and by the end of the decade, the Federal Emergency Management Agency (FEMA) had spent more than $25 billion to help alleviate suffering. In addition to natural disasters, FEMA agents assisted at the site of the Alfred P. Murrah Federal Building bombing on April 19, 1995, in Oklahoma City.

Beanie Babies Create a National Treasure Hunt

Launched by H. Ty Warner in 1993, Beanie Babies emerged as one of the hottest collectibles for kids and grown-ups alike. Seeing the need for a toy "in the $5 range that wasn't real garbage," Warner designed a whole series of small, under-stuffed, polyester plush toys filled with polyvinyl chloride pellets. Bypassing any kind of advertising campaign and refusing to court the big toy retailing giants such as Toys-R-Us, Warner instead shipped Beanie Babies to smaller retailers.

What really pushed the toys, such as "Flitter the Butterfly" or "Cheeks the Baboon," was that no single store carried the entire collection. As a result of that fact combined with Warner's "retirement" of certain toys after a short period of time on the market, the quest for the complete line of Beanie Babies became something akin to a treasure hunt with anxious collectors storming stores, advertising on the Internet, and stalking conventions in search of the ever-elusive Beanie to add to their collections. Prices for the rarer Beanies soared into the thousands of dollars with one retailer offering to sell the entire collection he had put together for $175,000. Sales for Warner's company reached $1 billion by 1999, making Warner one of the richest men in the country. On August 31,1999, Warner dropped the bombshell that as of December 31, 1999, his company would be retiring the line forever.

President Clinton Submits Sweeping Budget Cuts

President Clinton submitted his first budget in 1993, which included provisions to cut spending and increase taxes in order to decrease the budget deficit. It passed the House by a narrow margin of 219-213, and the Senate with a vote count of 50-49. Although Americans talked about the virtues of a limited government, they continued to expect a great deal for their tax dollars. With the end of the Cold War, Congress could no longer justify an enormous defense budget, and the Reagan Revolution had made regular tax cuts a political necessity.

Government spending, and thus services, had to contract. Communities that had depended on military bases and defense contracting faced economic hardship as bases were closed and spending programs curtailed. National parks were forced to cut back on services and started charging higher fees to visitors. Programs from the National Endowment for the Arts (NEA) to the National Aeronautics and Space Administration (NASA) scrambled to defend not only their spending but also their existence.

Hardest hit were the poor who bore the brunt of welfare and other spending reforms. Despite budgetary cutbacks, the government continued to respond to natural disasters. Victims of hurricanes along the Gulf Coast and the Carolinas, floods and droughts in the Midwest, and forest fires in the West found that agencies such as the Federal Emergency Management Administration (FEMA), the National Guard, and the Coast Guard were ready to help in the difficult and often dangerous tasks of rescue, recovery, and relief. Americans continued to criticize the government in general but appreciated the efforts of such agencies in times of need.

Artist Cindy Sherman Creates Controversial Images

In the 1990s critics and museum directors recognized Cindy Sherman as a major American artist when her work sold for record-high prices and *ARTnews* magazine included her on its list of the ten best living artists. In fact, Barbara Pollack of *ARTnews* magazine commented that Sherman "put a face on postmodernism."

Sherman gained critical acclaim in the late 1970s with her photo series titled *Untitled Film Stills* in which she satirized Hollywood stereotypes of women. She then gained widespread fame for her continued studies of gender stereotypes, and for the controversial 1993 Whitney Museum of American Art Biennial display for which she photographed mannequins with simulated genitalia to create, according to art critic Ralph Rug, "sexual scenarios rife with overtones of violation and brutality."

Her contribution to the 1995 biennial evolved into a more surreal presentation that was less sexual and more in line with Dada, with her noting, "I was sort of playing with the idea of violence. And I think that, as with some dada-ist photography, people might see a misogynist streak."

In 1997 Sherman directed *Office Killer*, a horror movie in which an office worker takes out her sexual frustrations by participating in a killing rampage. The movie starred Carol Kane and Molly Ringwald but did not garner much attention outside of art circles.

Sherman's show at the Metro Picture Gallery in New York City in 1999 used dolls and action figures in scenes of brutality and horror, which critics said lacked originality, though Pollack disagreed, writing that "Sherman subordinates herself as a work of eternal fiction—unknowable and ultimately absent from the artwork."

Hip-Hop Divides in Rivalries, and Two Superstars are Murdered

During the 1990s, massive changes occurred in the culture of hip-hop when musicians stripped away many of the original elements of the genre as rap music emerged. While rap music was a force in the 1980s with Run-DMC and LL Cool J spreading their Bronx sound from Brooklyn to Beverly Hills, few expected performers such as MC Hammer and Vanilla Ice to take rap to pop radio stations. By the 1990s, the authentic voice of inner-city youth became mindless and polished tunes that catered to suburban teens, losing its roots along the way.

However, numerous performers took rap back from the streets where it emerged, as street credibility became an essential part of the rap scene. Taking inspiration from pioneering rap artists like Public Enemy, West Coast musicians Dr. Dre and Ice Cube, from the dismantled N.W.A., convey messages of violence through "gangsta rap," which also had massive crossover appeal. Songs such as Ice Cube's "It Was a Good Day" in 1992 and Snoop Doggy Dogg's "Who I Am (What's My Name)" in 1993 were MTV and mainstream radio favorites. Snoop Doggy Dogg's album *Doggystyle* released in 1993 and became the first debut album to enter the pop-albums chart at number one.

As gangsta rap dominated the West, a new East Coast sound emerged. Positive-minded, Afrocentric groups brought intellectuality to the genre, as groups such as A Tribe Called Quest, De La Soul, Jungle Brothers, and Leaders of the New School formed an alliance called the Native Tongues, which focused on black history. Despite a few crossover tracks such as De La Soul's "Me, Myself, and I," East Coast rap remained underground while West Coast gangsta rap became commercialized.

In 1993-1994, two critical releases completely shifted rap fans' attention to the East. The first was the group Wu Tang Clan's debut album, *Enter the Wu Tang* in 1993. Led by rapper-producer RZA, the Wu Tang Clan had a hard, yet comical edge, and both RZA's production and creative lyrics pushed Wu Tang past other artists in terms of originality. A year later in April 1994, Nas's debut album, *Illmatic*, displayed a realistic portrait of street life. Both albums became commercial successes.

During the last half of the decade, a strong division developed between East and West Coast artists. Conflicts between the two groups were suggested as motives for the murders of its two leading stars and rivals, Tupac Shakur in 1996 and Notorious "Biggie Smalls" in 1997.

The Shifting Philosophy Regarding School Prayer

The "Establishment of Religion Clause" in the First Amendment of the U.S. Constitution prohibits Congress from establishing a national religion. For decades, the courts have fluctuated on the issue of prayer in schools. In 1984 Congress passed the Equal Access Act, which kept public schools from discriminating against students that wanted to meet at school for religious, political, or philosophical reasons. The law was challenged and reviewed by the Supreme Court in 1990. The Court upheld the law in *Board of Education v. Mergens*, declaring that the denial of a request made by a student for a Christian Bible club to meet in a public high school classroom violated the Act.

In *Lamb's Chapel v. Center Moriches Union Free School District* in 1993, the Court also held that any religious groups must be allowed the use of public-school facilities after hours if that access was granted to any other groups. Further lowering the wall between Church and State, the Court ruled in *Rosenberger v. University of Virginia* in 1995 that the choice by school administrators not to fund a student magazine written by a Christian group while providing funds for nonreligious publications violated the First Amendment. Justice David Hackett Souter dissented, arguing that "The Court today, for the first time, approves direct funding of core religious activities by an arm of the state."

Dallas Cowboys, San Francisco 49ers, and Denver Broncos Rule

The decade began with perennial powers the San Francisco 49ers, New York Giants, Washington Redskins, and Dallas Cowboys winning Super Bowls. Dallas won three (1993, 1994, and 1996) and San Francisco won two (1990 and 1995). The Giants in 1991 and Redskins in 1992 each won one, as did old school champions, the Green Bay Packers in 1997, their first title in 29 years. Their victory was widely hailed as a deserved reward for faithful fans and for three-time league MVP Brett Favre. The Denver Broncos and John Elway finally took the title in 1998. No American Football Conference (AFC) team, inexplicably, had won a Super Bowl since 1984, until Denver won two in a row, the second in 1999 against the Atlanta Falcons. The final season of the decade ended with the St. Louis Rams and Tennessee Titans heading to Super Bowl XXXIV (which was played on January 30, 2000, and won by the Rams).

20 RANDOM FACTS FROM 1993

1. On January 3, 1993, Russian President Boris Yeltsin and U.S. President George H. W. Bush sign the Start II Treaty that called for the elimination of two-thirds of the nuclear stockpiles of both nations.

2. On January 12, 1993, President Bill Clinton ordered the Attorney General to appoint a special counsel to investigate the Whitewater real estate dealings.

3. On January 20, 1993, Bill Clinton became the 42nd president of the United States.

4. On February 4, 1993, General Motors was found negligent by a jury in the faulty fuel-tank design that caused the death of a teenager. The jury awarded $105.2 million to the parents.

5. On February 24, 1993, the 35th Grammy Awards awarded *Unplugged* by Eric Clapton as Album of the Year and Clapton's song "Tears in Heaven" as Record of the Year.

6. In March 1993 the first issue of *Wired*, a magazine covering technology, was published.

7. On March 30, 1993, the 65th Academy Awards awarded *Unforgiven* as Best Picture, Emma Thompson as Best Actress for her role in *Howards End*, and Al Pacino as Best Actor for his role in *Scent of a Woman*.

8. On April 9, 1993, General Motors recalled millions of trucks that were regarded as hazardous.

9. On April 30, 1993, the European Organization for Nuclear Research announced that World Wide Web technology would be free to use by anyone.

10. On June 8, 1993, the Equal Employment Opportunity Commission (EEOC) ruled that employees could not refuse to hire disabled employees for reasons related to insurance costs.

11. On June 25, 1993, the Supreme Court ruled that employees must prove discrimination in all bias cases.

12. On July 27, 1993, IBM announced an $8.9 million plan to revive the company, which included the elimination of 60,000 jobs and a reduction in factories.

13. On August 10, 1993, Ruth Bader Ginsburg became the second woman to serve on the U.S. Supreme Court.

14. On November 2, 1993, the Dow Jones index hit a record 3,697.64.

15. On November 17, 1993, The House of Representatives approved the North Atlantic Free Trade Agreement (NAFTA), and four days later, the Senate approved the initiative.

16. On November 30, 1993, President Clinton signed the Brady Handgun Violence Prevention Act, which regulated firearm sales by requiring background checks for purchases.

17. In 1993 biochemists at the U.S. National Cancer Institute found one gene related to homosexuality.

18. In 1993 George Washington University researchers cloned human embryos and nurtured them in a Petri dish for several days, provoking protests from ethicists, politicians, and people opposed to genetic engineering.

19. In 1993 an international research team in Paris produced a rough map of all 23 pairs of human chromosomes.

20. In 1993 curbside recycling took off, resulting in an 85 percent increase over the number of communities that participated in recycling programs in the United States in 1988.

TEST YOUR 1993 KNOWLEDGE
10 QUESTIONS

1) Who was the leader of the Waco cult that was targeted by the Federal government?

   a) Randy Weaver
   b) David Koresh
   c) Timothy McVeigh

2) What collectible created a national treasure hunt in the mid-1990s?

   a) Beanie Babies
   b) Star Wars action figures
   c) Hot Wheels cars

3) Where was the mastermind of the 1993 World Trade Center found?

   a) New York City
   b) Jordan
   c) Pakistan

4) Artist Cindy Sherman used what main medium when creating her art pieces?

   a) Sculpture
   b) Oil paints
   c) Photography

5) The hip-hop alliance Native Tongues involved which set of performers?

   a) Dr. Dre, Ice Cube, and Snoop Doggy Dogg

    b) A Tribe Called Quest, De La Soul, and the Jungle Brothers

    c) Black Star, Jurassic 5, and the Black Eyed Peas

6) Which NFL team won the most Super Bowls in the 1990s?

    a) Dallas Cowboys
    b) San Francisco 49ers
    c) Denver Broncos

7) Which magazine made its debut in 1993?

    a) High Times
    b) Wired
    c) Spin

8) What new policy was required by the Brady Handgun Violence Protection Act?

    a) Background checks
    b) Elimination of gun silencers
    c) Elimination of clips that hold more than a dozen bullets

9) What experiment by George Washington University sparked protests?

    a) The finding of a gene related to homosexuality
    b) The cloning of headless mice
    c) The cloning of human embryos

10) What activity increased by 85 percent from 1988 to 1993 in the U.S.?

    a) Curbside recycling
    b) Alcohol consumption
    c) Drug overdose deaths

ANSWERS

1) b

2) a

3) c

4) c

5) b

6) a

7) b

8) a

9) c

10) a

CHAPTER FIVE
1994

MAJOR EVENTS

John Wayne Bobbitt Temporarily Loses an Appendage

On January 21, 1994, in Manassas, Virginia, John Wayne Bobbitt reported to police that his wife, Lorena, had amputated his penis while he slept and threw it away while driving from the couple's home. It was later recovered, put on ice, and taken to the hospital where the appendage was reattached. John Wayne Bobbitt was later acquitted of marital sexual assault; Lorena was acquitted of malicious wounding by reason of insanity. The two became tabloid sensations for the whole next year.

Brady Handgun Violence Protection Act

The Brady Handgun Violence protection Act was named after Sarah Brady, antigun lobbyist and wife of James Brady, who was severely injured by a bullet from a handgun during the Reagan assassination attempt. It was signed into law on November 30, 1993, and went into effect on February 28, 1994.

The Brady Law established a national five-business-day waiting period, or a "cooling off" interlude, and required local law enforcement to conduct background checks on handgun purchasers. The waiting period applied only to handgun sales through licensed dealers. Transfers between private individuals, as well as sales at gun shows and through the Internet, were not included. Within one day of the proposed transfer, a dealer is required to provide information from the purchaser's statement to the chief law enforcement officer where the purchaser resides.

The 1994 Lillehammer Winter Olympics

Like much else in sports, the decision to separate the Summer and Winter Olympics by a span of two years was driven by financial considerations. It made more sense to produce such a massive event, with television broadcasting rights and a host of other commercial interests at stake, every two years rather than both Games separated by a mere few months every four years.

The Americans performed as usual, winning six gold medals at Lillehammer and placing fifth once again in total medals in essentially the same events with the same cast of characters in the spotlight, but for different reasons. Figure skater Nancy Kerrigan, victim of an attack against her for the sole purpose of reducing her chances of winning her event, valiantly trained and returned to the Olympics to give a silver-medal performance. Tonya Harding, who would later plead guilty to a charge of hindering the investigation, sued for the right to compete in the Olympic figure-skating competition, and subsequently placed eighth.

The other repeat performer from the 1992 Winter Olympics was Bonnie Blair for which this was her fourth Olympiad. Again, she won the 500- and 1,000-meter women's long track speed skating gold medals, bringing her total number of Olympic victories to five. Dan Jansen, a sentimental favorite after having been thwarted in his previous attempts, won the men's long track 1,000-meter speed skating race. He took an emotional lap with baby daughter Jane, who he named after his sister whose death he had learned immediately prior to his Olympic competition in 1988. Alaskan Tommy Moe won the men's downhill in Alpine skiing.

Nine Inch Nails, Alanis Morissette, and Illicit Lyrics

Many performers in the 1990s used sexually explicit lyrics to sell albums. Trent Reznor of Nine Inch Nails defended his group's lyrics by saying, "When I'm on stage singing—screaming this primal scream—I look at the audience, and everyone else is screaming the lyrics back at me. Even though what I'm saying appears negative, the release of it becomes a positive kind of experience, I think, and provides some catharsis to other people."

Alanis Morissette, who began her music career as a performer in the Canadian Tulip Festivals before becoming a teen dance party star, was far removed from those naïve roots by 1994 when her album *Jagged Little Pill* expressed her deepest and most tortured emotions in often-illicit ways. Her songs explored sexuality, relationship failures, negative feelings toward the Catholic Church, and other aspects of individual identity crises. Within six weeks of its release, her album had reached number 10 on the Billboard albums chart, based upon the strength of its lead single "You Oughta Know." Morissette's album remained on the chart for an entire year, won her six Grammy Awards, and became the best-selling U.S. debut album of all time by a female solo artist.

Screen Violence and the Associated Backlash

In the films of the 1990s, violence was prevalent and graphic, and many educators and politicians expressed their concerns about the connection between violent movies and increasing levels of violence in schools.

For example, Oliver Stone's *Natural Born Killers*, released in 1994, follows a pair of serial-killing sociopaths, played by Woody Harrelson and Juliette Lewis, who go on a cross-country killing spree. The movie sparked copycat murders by teenagers who claimed that the movie provided them with inspiration for their crimes. Furthermore, the shootings at Columbine High School in April 1999 drew similar comparisons to those portrayed in the 1995 movie *The Basketball Diaries*, which involved a trench-coat-clad character with a machine gun attacking people who had mocked him. The argument against movies like *Natural Born Killers* (1994), *The Basketball Diaries* (1995), and *Kalifornia* (1993), which involved serial killers, was that the plots seemed to celebrate purposeless violence in a provocative and romantic fashion.

While concerned citizens began to discuss the difference between the justifiable violence portrayed in films like *Saving Private Ryan* and the unacceptable violence found in *Natural Born Killers*, some critics noted redeeming qualities in the movie, including Roger Ebert. Ebert said that the movie is not about two murders; instead, it is "about the way they electrify the media and exhilarate the public," as the film exposes American society's morally bankrupt obsession with violence and celebrity.

Judge Rules that Microsoft is a Monopoly

In a 207-page ruling by Judge Thomas Penfield Jackson in the lawsuit *United States of America v. Microsoft Corporation*, he stated that under the control of CEO William Henry "Bill" Gates III, Microsoft was a monopoly, which is not in itself illegal, but it had improperly abused its power to the detriment of competitors and consumers. The charges against the company, which controlled more than 90 percent of the computer software market and had a market value of $470 billion by 1999, represented serious violations of law. The judge's finding of facts alleged that Microsoft constricted its web browser competitor Netscape's access to the market by bundling its own browser, Microsoft Internet Explorer, with the popular computer operating system Microsoft Windows. This meant that all computer systems that used Windows contained Microsoft's own browser, thereby making the Netscape browser technically unnecessary.

Agreeing with the Justice Department's lead attorney Joel I. Klein, the Court also found that Microsoft had used strong-arm tactics by including its browser on Apple Computers and bullied computer-chip maker Intel into staying out of the software market. In addition to its aggressive approach to competitors, Judge Jackson further noted that by bundling the Explorer browser with the Windows operating system, Microsoft harmed consumers. Jackson found that this practice slowed down the operating system, increased the likelihood of system failures, and made the software more susceptible to viruses.

In its defense, Microsoft attorneys argued that the company's practices were competitive but not illegal. However, on July 15, 1994, Microsoft promised to end practices used to corner the market.

The 25th Anniversary of Woodstock is Commemorated

On August 12-14, 1994, Woodstock '94 took place to commemorate the 25th anniversary of the original Woodstock. It was held at Winston Farms in Saugerties, New York, and was plagued by days of rain that created a giant mud pit at the venue. The event cost $135 and a pay-per-view package for home viewing ran $49.

More than 50 bands played to 350,000 attendees. Green Day and Nine Inch Nails stole the show and were joined by classic rockers like Santana and the highlight of the festival, Bob Dylan.

An Instant Classic Finds Redemption

Amidst the ongoing discussion regarding violence in the film industry, a classic was born in 1994. *The Shawshank Redemption*, a movie about hope, love, friendship, and survival, was a prison drama filled with its own brand of violence that was never gratuitous.

The movie was adapted from a novella by Stephen King, and actor Tim Robbins played Andy Dufresne, a banker who is condemned to life in prison at a maximum-security facility for the murder of his wife and her lover.

Dufresne claims innocence as he lives through beatings and sexual propositions, but with the help of another inmate, played by Morgan Freeman, he learns to survive through intelligence and hard work. All the while, he continues to hold out hope that he will be free one day, believing that "Fear can hold you prisoner. Hope can set you free." While it added to the brutality of the decade, Roger Ebert said that *The Shawshank Redemption* "is not about violence, riots, or melodrama. The word 'redemption' is in the title for a reason." Andy's final redemption is both physical and spiritual.

Trouble in Dallas

Once America's Team, the Dallas Cowboys seemed to be despised by many fans during the decade. Callers to radio sports-talk shows, and for that matter, sportswriters and commentators, could not show enough contempt for owner Jerry Jones and coach Barry Switzer. At the end of the 1980s, Jones had brought in Jimmy Johnson from the University of Miami Hurricanes to coach his team, and Johnson led the Cowboys to two consecutive championships. A series of off-the-field activities by his players, however, ranging from accusations of drug use to battery, some of which were later discovered to be false, stained the image of the team.

Jones did not help himself either in the eyes of management when he defied the NFL by signing sponsorship deals with Pepsi and Nike that broke the spirit and letter of league rules. Then, in a feud with Johnson, Jones fired his successful coach and hired renegade Oklahoma University coach Switzer, who had enough coaching skills and player talent to win one more Super Bowl before moving on from his own mutually disagreeable relationship with Jones.

The World Series is Cancelled

Major league baseball went from the depths of despair to a nearly full recovery during the 1990s. Felipe Alou, coach of the Montreal Expos, said, "Sometimes, something has to almost die, like baseball did, for the miracle to take place." Greed and money nearly caused the downfall of the sport. Strikes and work stoppages were nothing new to professional sports, and baseball had experienced its share of both, befitting its rank as the eldest of major league athletic enterprises in the United States. However, never had a World Series been canceled as it was in 1994 because of a 272-day strike by players that forced the cancellation of 920 games. The contest between owners and players focused on salary caps and revenue sharing. When baseball finally resumed, it did so amidst fan animosity directed at players, owners, and baseball in general.

20 RANDOM FACTS FROM 1994

1. On January 1, 1994, NAFTA went into effect.

2. On January 7, 1994, the unemployment rate fell to a three-year low of 6.4 percent.

3. On January 24, 1994, the Dow Jones closed above 3,900 for the first time, ending the day at 3,914.48.

4. On January 17, 1994, an earthquake in Northridge, California, registered 6.6 on the Richter scale, resulting in the deaths of 61 people.

5. On February 3, 1994, President Clinton ended the trade embargo against the Republic of Vietnam, which had been in effect since 1975.

6. On February 4, 1994, the Federal Reserve increased interest rates for the first time in five years, which triggered a huge sell-off on Wall Street.

7. On March 1, 1994, the 36th Grammy Awards awarded Album of the Year for the soundtrack *The Bodyguard* by Whitney Houston and other artists and Record of the Year for Houston's "I Will Always Love You."

8. On March 21, 1994, the 66th Academy Awards presented *Shindler's List* the Best Picture award, Holly Hunter the Best Actress award for her role in *The Piano*, and Tommy Lee Jones the Best Actor award for his role in *The Fugitive.*

9. On April 4, 1994, Netscape Communications was founded.

10. On April 22, 1994, former U.S. President Nixon died in a New York City hospital.

11. On May 6, 1994, Paula Jones filed suit in a federal court and charged that President Clinton committed sexual harassment against her while he was governor of Arkansas.

12. On May 10, 1994, convicted serial killer John Wayne Gacy, Jr., who had killed 33 young men and boys in the 1970s, was executed by lethal injection in Illinois.

13. On May 24, 1994, the United States and Japan agreed to revive efforts that would open Japanese markets to U.S. goods.

14. On August 3, 1994, Stephen Gerald Breyer was sworn in as an Associate Justice of the U.S. Supreme Court of the United States.

15. In November 1994 a math professor discovered a flaw in Intel's new Pentium processor, and as a result, the flaw ended up costing the company more than $475 million; Intel vowed to replace all faulty processors.

16. On November 6, 1994, the Republicans swept the midterm elections, taking control of both houses of the U.S. Congress.

17. On December 5, 1994, "Newt" Gingrich was chosen as Speaker of the House.

18. On December 6, 1994, Webster L. Hubbell, Associate Attorney General of the United States, pleaded guilty to tax evasion and mail fraud. He spent 18 months in prison.

19. In 1994 scientists discovered three planets orbiting the dim remnants of a star that exploded long ago, evidence of a solar system beyond our own.

20. In 1994 the revised open-source operating system Linux 1.0 was released over the Internet.

TEST YOUR 1994 KNOWLEDGE
10 QUESTIONS

1) What did John Wayne Bobbitt lose in a domestic dispute?

   a) His life
   b) His penis
   c) His children

2) Which violent movie did some say inspired the Columbine school shooting?

   a) *Natural Born Killers*
   b) *Kalifornia*
   c) *The Basketball Diaries*

3) Which technology company was accused of being a monopoly in the 1990s?

   a) Apple
   b) American Online (AOL)
   c) Microsoft

4) Which festival saw a revival in 1994?

   a) The Sundance Film Festival
   b) Woodstock
   c) Ozzfest

5) What sporting event was cancelled because of a 272-day strike by the players in its league?

   a) World Series
   b) NBA Finals
   c) Super Bowl

6) Which former U.S. President died in 1994?

   a) Richard Nixon
   b) Gerald Ford
   c) Lyndon B. Johnson

7) Who was Paula Jones?

   a) She was involved in the Whitewater controversy
   b) She accused Bill Clinton of sexual harassment
   c) She had an affair with Bill Clinton

8) Which serial killer was executed in 1994?

   a) John Wayne Gacy
   b) Jeffery Dahmer
   c) Henry Lee Lucas

9) Which open-source operating system was released in 1994?

   a) Netscape
   b) Linux
   c) World Wide Web

10) Who became the U.S. Speaker of the House in 1994?

   a) Newt Gingrich
   b) Bob Dole
   c) Stephan Gerald Breyer

ANSWERS

1) b

2) c

3) c

4) b

5) a

6) a

7) b

8) a

9) b

10) a

CHAPTER SIX
1995

MAJOR EVENTS

O.J. Simpson and the Trial of the Century

Three years after the Rodney King beating, Los Angeles and the nation were once again polarized by racial divisions over a jury verdict. This time, however, the individual acquitted was Orenthal James "O. J." Simpson, a retired football star, sports announcer, television personality, and the prime suspect in the murders of his former wife, Nicole Brown Simpson, and her friend Ronald Goldman on June 12, 1994. Simpson, an African American, was arrested on June 17, 1994, after a lengthy televised car chase on the Los Angeles freeway; both of the victims were white.

In a July Gallup Poll, 64 percent of black respondents believed Simpson would not receive a fair trial, while only 41 percent of whites held that opinion. By the time a grand was convened to review the evidence and determine if an indictment was warranted, Simpson had hired a cadre of celebrity lawyers, including Johnnie L. Cochran, Jr.; F. Lee Bailey; Robert Shapiro; and appeals expert Alan M. Dershowitz. The group was referred to by the media as the "Dream Team."

The People of California v. Orenthal James Simpson was called the "trial of the century" and made celebrities of many participants in the case, including judge Lance A. Ito. Several important judicial issues emerged, including the growing use of technology in judicial proceedings, the merits and problems of live television in the courtroom, and the reliability of DNA evidence, as well as more traditional problems, such as the use of race as a defense tactic. In a much-debated move, Ito decided that the trial could be televised.

The Simpson trial began on January 23, 1995, with hundreds of reporters from all over the world camped out in front of the courthouse. The jury consisted of eight blacks, two Hispanics, one white, and one person of mixed race; eight women, four men. The prosecution team, led by attorneys Marcia Clark, Christopher Darden (the only black on the team), and William Hodgman, portrayed Simpson as abusive (several years earlier he had pleaded no contest to abusing his wife), jealous, and controlling. The evidence, however, was largely circumstantial; there was no weapon and there were no witnesses that directly linked the defendant to the crimes, but the prosecution presented a series of DNA experts who testified that blood found at the crime scene matched Simpson's DNA profile.

The defense argued that Simpson did not have the opportunity to commit the crimes, that his demeanor before and after the murders was not consistent with that of a murderer, and that the evidence presented was not only circumstantial but may also have been planted, particularly by Mark Fuhrman, a police detective whose history of racism was demonstrated in a series of audiotapes in which he used racial epithets. This evidence provided the Dream Team with the opportunity to introduce the so-called "race card." Over fellow defense attorney Shapiro's objections, Cochran suggested to the majority-black jury that there was a widespread conspiracy against African Americans in the justice system. He even compared Simpson, a murder defendant, with Rodney King, a victim of police brutality.

On October 2, 1995, Judge Ito referred the case to the jury. At this time, even given the problems that plagued the prosecution, public-opinion polls indicated that more than half of Americans believed Simpson was guilty of the crimes. Whites were four times more likely than blacks, however, to hold this belief. Three hours and forty minutes after receiving the case, the jury reached a verdict. Fearing a replay of the civil disturbance after the 1992 King verdict, the judge delayed the reading until the next day to give the police department time to prepare. On October 3, with millions of Americans watching television or to listening to radio, the verdict was announced. Simpson was found not guilty.

Simpson's legal troubles did not end with the criminal trial. The following year the families of Nicole Brown Simpson and Ronald Goldman filed a civil suit against Simpson. Unlike the criteria for determining a verdict in the criminal trial, a civil verdict has the lower criterion of "preponderance of evidence" rather than "beyond reasonable doubt." This trial lasted three months. A jury unanimously declared that Simpson was financially liable for the deaths. The families were awarded $8.2 million in compensatory damages and another $25 million in punitive damages.

Newt Gingrich Sets the Republican Political Agenda

Newton Leroy "Newt" Gingrich burst onto the political scene in 1979 as a brash young Republican congressperson from Georgia who was unwilling to quietly take his seat on the backbenches of the minority party while waiting for sufficient seniority to accrue and allow for him to be influential. He wanted influence immediately and his ambitions for himself and the Republican Party were unconcealed. He wanted to help develop a Republican majority in the House, and his personal ambition was to become Speaker of the House, which was his title from 1995-1998. From the outset, he clashed with congressional stalwarts from both parties. He was a new order politician—impatient, willing to step on colleagues' toes, and innovative.

He entered the House in 1979 at a time when there was a profound sense that the United States was directionless and that its people were hungry for new leadership. This view was reinforced by the election of Ronald Reagan to the presidency and a Republican majority in the Senate in 1980. Reagan's victory had failed to translate into Republican success in the House, however, and control of the House remained in Democratic hands throughout the 1980s and early 1990s. In fact, Republicans had suffered further losses in the House in the 1982 election. Over the next dozen years, Gingrich organized a movement and developed a political organization that led to a Republican majority in the House after the 1994 elections, propelled him to Speaker, and profoundly changed the fundamental assumptions and content of American politics for the remainder of the decade.

Gingrich brought a new style to American politics— media-savvy, in-your-face, partisanship, and ideological. It has become the mainstay of much of the business of Congress, especially in the House; it sparked a national debate about the decline of civility in American political discourse. Furthermore, he was responsible for setting the political agenda that made the Republican Party the majority party in the House after four frustrating decades of wandering in the political wilderness of seemingly perpetual minority status. His "Contract with America" enjoyed some very real successes, notably in welfare reform, and the issues it raised remained a fundamental part of the American political landscape at the end of the decade.

Pop-Country and Women Dominate the Country Charts

Country music moved closer to mainstream pop music in the 1990s, and new female vocalists such as Shania Twain, Faith Hill, LeAnn Rimes, and the Dixie Chicks led the charge, along with male country artists such as Garth Brooks, Steve Earle, Alan Jackson, Marty Stuart, and Tim McGraw. Many traditionalists charged that country music was losing its sense of history as many of the top country stars of the 1970s and 1980s disappeared from the charts.

Country music during the 1990s saw the emergence of new female stars that included Canadian Shania Twain, who would have been called a pop-country crossover singer in the 1980s but in the 1990s was considered New Country. In 1995 her second album *The Woman in Me* sold more than 11 million copies in the United States, with four singles from the album topping the country charts, while the album made its way to the top of the pop charts. By the end of the decade, her next album *Come On Over* had sold 16 million copies.

After the success of her 1996 debut album *Blue*, 13-year-old LeAnn Rimes became the youngest singer to ever be nominated for a Country Music Award. She won two Grammys the following year for Best New Artist and Best Country Performance.

Alison Krauss also earned a large and loyal following through her sensitive lyrics and deep music. In 1993, at the age of 21, she became the youngest member of the Grand Ole Opry. Her 1995 album *Now That I've Found You: A Collection* sold two million copies. Her two other albums *Every Time You Say Goodbye* in 1992 and *So Long So Wrong* in 1997 won Grammys for Best Bluegrass Album. By the end of the 1990s, she had won ten Grammys and four Country Music Association Awards.

Comet Hale-Bopp Provides a Show, and Another Hits Jupiter

On July 22, 1995, two men independently discovered a previously unknown comet at about the same time. Alan Hale, a professional astronomer, saw the comet from his home in Southern New Mexico, while Tom Bopp, an amateur stargazer, saw it from the Arizona desert. Named after the two men, it is known as Comet Hale-Bopp. Scientists soon determined that the comet—a chunk of streaming ice, chemicals, and dust on a multi-millennial trip around the sun—was going to provide a great show for people on Earth.

Estimated to have a nucleus 25 miles in diameter and a tail several million miles long, Hale-Bopp was thought to be the biggest and brightest comet to have come near the Earth since 1811. Though it came no closer to Earth than 122 million miles, it was easily visible to the naked eye throughout much of 1997. It was not expected to return near Earth for more than two thousand years.

In 1994 Comet Shoemaker-Levy 9 provided the opening act for Hale-Bopp when, over the course of a week, its broken fragments crashed into Jupiter, the collisions visible to backyard astronomers on Earth. Shoemaker-Levy 9 provided scientists with their first opportunity to watch a comet collide with a planet, giving them an idea of what could happen if a comet was to crash into Earth.

Amazon Founder Jeff Bezos Pioneers Internet Commerce

The Bezos family traces its American roots to Colonel Robert Hall, who moved to San Antonio, Texas, at the beginning of the 19th Century from their home in Tennessee, and later to Bernhardt Vesper, Jeff Bezos's great-great grandfather, who purchased a ranch in the southern part of Texas. The 25,000-acre oasis in Cotulla was where Jeff Bezos spent his summers as a child.

Bezos was born on January 12, 1964, when his mother Jackie was only 17 years old. Bezos never knew his biological father; instead, Mike Bezos, a Cuban refugee who came to the United States without family at the age of 15, married Jeff's mother and raised Jeff as his own son. The pioneering spirit is part of the Bezos's bloodline, even if Jeff's new frontier was established in the realm of cyberspace.

Bezos's moment of insight came in 1994, in the early days of the Internet, while sitting in front of his computer in the office of his Midtown Manhattan office. Bezos went to a website that measured Internet use, and to his surprise, he discovered that the Internet was growing at a rate of 2,300 percent a year. "It was a wake-up call," he recalled. "I started thinking, what kind of business opportunity might there be here?"

On July 16, 1995, Bezos started Amazon.com to sell books, but his ambition was much greater. He wanted to own the biggest store in the world, a place that sold all things. "Anything," Bezos proclaimed, "with a capital A." Bezos's notion that the Internet would revolutionize commerce was considered visionary and outrageous at the time. Many critics wondered how long his finances and investors would hold, especially since he had posted a net loss of $350 million in 1999.

However, Bezos did not listen to his critics because he was convinced that as the volume of customers on

Amazon.com increased, he could lower prices and eliminate his competition, and investors agreed. At the end of 1999, Amazon stock was $94 per share with annual sales near $1 billion.

Cal Ripken Becomes Major League Baseball's Iron Man

Salvation came for the MLB after its long strike and 1994 World Series cancellation, specifically, on September 6, 1995, at Camden Yards in Baltimore, Maryland, when Cal Ripken, Jr., one of the most respected baseball veterans, broke Lou Gehrig's long-held, much-cherished record for consecutive games played. Everything came together when his attempt to break the standard became a media event of the first rank. Unlike a new record that could pop up randomly, Ripken's assault on the Iron Man's historic mark of consecutive games played, which Gehrig had achieved during the 1925-1939 baseball seasons, created the perfect opportunity for a national countdown.

For even more dramatic effect, the record was not actually bested when Ripken stepped on the field or when the umpire yelled, "Play ball." The game needed to be played for at least four and one-half innings in order to be official and recorded for posterity. Simply exiting the dugout and doffing his cap after breaking the record did not pacify the fans, so Ripken trotted the circumference of the field, shaking hands and touching fans in the stadium for a half-hour while play was halted, and America rejoiced at this revalidation of its favorite pastime. The play-by-play announcers had the good sense to be silent and let the drama speak for itself. Parents called their children to the television set, and Americans watched as one man—by sheer perseverance, goodwill, and charm—single-handedly revived a sport that had been deathly ill. He also hit a sixth-inning homerun, which dispelled any notion that his streak was an act of generosity or a public relations ploy on the part of management.

Ripken eventually played in 2,632 consecutive games, ending the streak when he benched himself on September 19, 1998, during which time a total of 266 players were utilized by the Baltimore Orioles. An American League starter in every All-Star Game beginning in 1984 through the end of his career, Ripken held the record for career home runs as a shortstop with 345 at the end of the decade. He was voted league MVP in 1983 and 1991.

Teen Pop and the Buying Power of Kids

"Blissfully nonjudgmental" was one description of teen music fans in the 1990s. If a single had a tempo and was danceable, teenagers would buy it, especially if the recording artist had style and looks. Britney Spears had it all figured out. Her career in entertainment started when she earned a part in an off-Broadway production of *Ruthless* in 1991, and the following year at the age of ten, she joined the cast of the *Mickey Mouse Club* on the Disney Channel. When the show was canceled in 1993, she signed a recording contract with Jive Records, and in 1999, seventeen-year-old Spears became a pop idol with her hit single "Baby One More Time."

With a sophisticated harmony and nice melodies, the Backstreet Boys became the most popular all-male group of the late 1990s. They had seven platinum singles from their album *Millennium* in 1999, and tickets for their fall 1999 concert tour sold out in just one hour on August 17, grossing $30 million.

The vocal sensation Hanson, which was made up of three brothers, had a major hit single with "MMMBop" in 1997. After they appeared on the Nickelodeon Kids' Choice Awards, which has a viewing audience of 6- to 12-year-olds, their album *In the Middle of Nowhere* moved from 63 to 36 on the Billboard albums chart in a day, before going on to sell 10 million copies worldwide.

The success of these teen idols demonstrated the spending power of kids. Children influenced $50 billion a year in household spending in the 1990s and had more disposable income than ever before. "Kids are a little bit more mature at a younger age today," said Nickelodeon VP of talent Paula Kaplan, indicating parents were more aware of their children's material needs and "more involved in what their kids are doing. I think parents and kids alike listen to pop music groups like Hanson, Spice Girls, and the Backstreet Boys."

Cyberporn, the Pitfall on the Information Superhighway

The Internet provided quick and easy worldwide access to information for people both at home and at the office beginning in the 1990s. Bright entrepreneurs developed various e-commerce sites, and the web became a viable place of business for many, including those offering sexually explicit images. Unlike seedy adult bookstores, many pornographic sites in cyberspace are easily accessible to anyone at a computer keyboard, including children. That recognition set off a raging debate about the legality of pornography on the web. At the core of this debate was the question raised by the new technology—was the web more like print media and therefore protected by the First Amendment from being over-regulated, or was it more like broadcast media and subject to stricter federal regulation and oversight?

New technologies made pornography on the web accessible and profitable. "Adult" sites on the web were a billion-dollar business by 1998, and more than half of the search engine requests were adult-oriented. While many pornographic sites required identification and a credit card, many others could be accessed by anyone with web service. One survey found that 25 percent of teens said they had visited X-rated websites. Almost all online consumers of porn were men, and a great deal of the adult material available consisted of images not readily available in the average porn magazine market— including bondage, sadomasochism, bestiality, and pedophilia.

When cyberporn gained attention and became subjected to a wider public awareness in the mid-1990s, the U.S. House and Senate voted overwhelmingly in favor of the Communications Decency Act, which called for two years in prison and fines up to $250,000 for any display of "patently offensive material" that could be viewed by a minor.

Tabloid Journalism and the Death of Princess Diana

In the 1990s, the line between serious journalism and tabloid reporting blurred substantially. Supermarket tabloids such as the *National Enquirer*, *Star*, and *Weekly World News* broke and reported top news stories, and more and more, the stories that appeared in print and television news began to look like reports from the *National Enquirer*. In fact, *Inside Edition* won a Polk Award for a piece about the abuses perpetuated by the insurance industry in Arkansas, and major networks provided almost nonstop coverage of the woes of Michael Jackson, O. J. Simpson, Patsy and John Ramsey, and Bill Clinton.

News anchor Dan Rather called this trend toward the sensational "news light." On the one hand, for example, Americans assailed the journalistic world for reporting the sordid details of Clinton's sex scandal, and yet they clamored for more, seemingly not able to get enough of them. The decade ended with debates still raging about journalistic ethics and the intrusion of the press into the private lives of public figures.

Diana, Princess of Wales, had often complained about the paparazzi who seemed to follow her everywhere after she first came to public attention when she was courted by Prince Charles and then continued unabated when she married him. When she died in a car accident in Paris on August 31, 1997, while being chased by photographers, her plight raised public interest and anger over the ways news was gathered.

President Bill Clinton Impeachment

In November 1995 President Clinton began an affair with White House intern Monica S. Lewinsky. Coupled with allegations of adultery throughout his political career, his moral integrity was on the line during most of his presidency, but it wasn't until he was accused of obstructing justice that his troubles really began.

The Clinton administration coincided with one of the longest periods of U.S. economic expansion in history. In an economy powered by a growing technology sector and low gasoline prices, unemployment fell and inflation remained negligible. Deficit spending, which had grown enormously in the 1980s, was replaced with a budget surplus. President Clinton arguably should have been the most popular executive since Dwight D. Eisenhower and might have been had his personal life not tarnished his reputation.

Even as a Rhodes Scholar at Oxford University, Clinton had been plagued with rumors of sexual misbehavior. As governor of Arkansas, he allegedly sexually harassed a young woman named Paula Corbin Jones. Such allegations might have gone nowhere had he and his wife, Hillary Rodham Clinton, not become caught up in a failed land deal called Whitewater while he was still Arkansas' governor.

Kenneth W. Starr, appointed under the former independent prosecutor law to investigate the Whitewater affair, found instead, the young, unpaid intern Lewinsky, who had become involved sexually with the president. When Clinton apparently lied to a grand jury about his relationship with Lewinsky, Starr pressed the House of Representatives to impeach the president. After extensive and heavily televised hearings, the House voted to impeach, mostly along party lines. While most Americans condemned the president's behavior, they saw the impeachment proceedings as a politically motivated attempt at a coup. In the midterm elections of 1998, in the midst of the impeachment crisis, the Republicans lost ground. Gingrich, taking responsibility for the defeat, resigned his House seat.

The Senate, nevertheless, tried the case but failed to convict; Clinton's legacy, and perhaps the presidency, was besmirched by the process. Critics predicted that Clinton would be crippled by the impeachment and unable to govern effectively during his last two years in office. Yet, ever the "Comeback Kid," he put the issue behind him and continued to lead effectively. The country prospered, and many Americans acknowledged that, while disapproving of his personal behavior, they could not argue with the results of his governance.

20 RANDOM FACTS FROM 1995

1. On January 1, 1995, the World Trade Organization (WTO) came into existence with 81 member countries.

2. On January 11, 1995, Pope John Paul II began an 11-day tour of Asia and Australia, and four million people attended his open-air mass in Manila on the 15th.

3. On January 17, 1995, more than 5,000 people died in an earthquake in Kobe, Japan.

4. On January 31, 1995, severe flooding impacted large areas of Northern Europe, and in the Netherlands alone, 200,000 people were evacuated from their homes.

5. On February 26, 1995, the oldest merchant bank in Britain, Baring's, collapsed after the loss of 600 million pounds.

6. On February 28, 1995, U.S. and Italian troops began the evacuation of 1,500 UN troops from Somalia after warring factions refused to abide to a ceasefire.

7. On March 1, 1995, the 37th Grammy Awards awarded Album of the Year to the album *MTV Unplugged: Tony Bennett* and Record of the Year to Sheryl Crow for "All I Wanna Do."

8. On March 20, 1995, terrorists released the nerve gas sarin in a Tokyo subway, killing 12 and

injuring 5,000. Aum Shinrikyo cult leader Shoko Asahara was arrested on May 15 in connection with attack.

9. On March 27, 1995, the 67th Academy Awards awarded *Forrest Gump* for Best Picture and Tom Hanks as Best Actor for his role in the movie. Jessica Lang won Best Actress for her role in *Blue Sky*.

10. On March 28, 1995, the UN World Climate Conference opened in Berlin with delegates from more than 130 nations in attendance.

11. On April 22, 1995, the Tutsi-led Rwanda Patriotic Army killed 2,000 Hutu refugees at a camp in Southern Rwanda.

12. On May 10, 1995, in Zaire, health officials reported that an outbreak of the deadly Ebola virus had claimed many lives.

13. On May 25, 1995, NATO warplanes bombed Bosnian Serb targets after the Serbs refused to relinquish control of their heavy weapons to peacekeeping forces. The next day, the Bosnian Serbs seized UN soldiers as hostages.

14. On May 30-31, 1995, the Prince of Wales toured the Republic of Ireland in the first royal visit since 1911.

15. On August 21, 1995, Shannon Faulkner became the first woman to attend The Citadel, a state-supported all-male military college in Charleston, South Carolina, in its Corp of Cadets. She dropped out of school on August 18th.

16. On September 28, 1995, Israeli Prime Minister Yitzhak Rabin and PLO chairman Yasser Arafat signed an accord in Washington, D.C., transferring much of the West Bank to Palestinian control.

17. In December 1995 the White House and Congressional Republicans jousted over the national budget, which resulted in the longest federal shutdown in U.S. history, continuing 21 days, and didn't end until January 6, 1996.

18. On December 14, 1995, the presidents of Bosnia, Serbia, and Croatia formally signed a peace accord, ending a conflict which had claimed 200,000 lives and left 3 million homeless.

19. On December 20, 1995, 60,000 NATO peacekeeping troops began Operation Joint Endeavor in Bosnia after warring parties signed an agreement to end the four-year conflict in Bosnia-Herzegovina.

20. In December 1995, the hottest year to date was recorded by scientists, signaling to many, a sign of global warming.

TEST YOUR 1995 KNOWLEDGE
10 QUESTIONS

1) Who was the most dominate female country musician by record sales in the 1990s?

   a) Faith Hill
   b) Shania Twain
   c) Alison Kraus

2) Who was the judge in the O.J. Simpson trial?

   a) Judge Judy Sheindlin
   b) Judge Joseph Wapner
   c) Judge Lance Ito

3) Who set the agenda for the Republican Party for the last half of the 1990s?

   a) Bob Dole
   b) Newt Gingrich
   c) Ronald Reagan

4) Which comet made its debut in 1995?

   a) Comet Hale-Bopp
   b) Halley's Comet
   c) Comet Lovejoy

5) Who started Amazon.com in the 1990s?

   a) Steve Jobs
   b) Paul Allen
   c) Jeff Bezos

6) Who was called baseball's "Iron Man"?

   a) Cal Ripken
   b) Sammy Sosa
   c) Mark McGwire

7) Which group had the hit single "MMMBop"?

   a) Backstreet Boys
   b) Boyz II Men
   c) Hanson

8) Which famous person died in a car crash while being chased by the paparazzi?

   a) Kurt Cobain
   b) Princess Diana
   c) Dano Plato

9) Which military college admitted a female student for the first time in 1995?

   a) United States Naval Academy
   b) The Citadel
   c) Virginia Military Institute

10) Where did Operation Joint Endeavor occur?

   a) Rwanda
   b) Croatia
   c) Bosnia

ANSWERS

1) b

2) c

3) b

4) a

5) c

6) a

7) c

8) b

9) b

10) c

CHAPTER SEVEN
1996

MAJOR EVENTS

The Unabomber is Captured

One of the longest violent-crime cases of the Federal Bureau of Investigation (FBI), which was active for seventeen years, involved a series of fatal bombings. It was called the Unabomb case, a code name selected because some of the bombs were set off on university campuses and another was placed aboard an airliner. Beginning in 1978, the serial bomber, later identified as Theodore John Kaczynski, mailed or placed 16 homemade explosive devices, killing 3 persons and injuring 23 others. A crucial development in the case occurred in early 1996 when the bomber sent a manuscript to *The New York Times* and *Washington Post*. With FBI approval, both papers published the 35,000-word treatise. The Unabomber argued that the purpose of the bombings was to call attention to the destabilizing effects of technology and "leftism" on modern society and traditional values. Publication of the manifesto led David Kaczynski to link it with earlier writings of his estranged brother Ted, who was living as a recluse near a small town in Montana.

On April 3, 1996, Ted Kaczynski, a former mathematics

professor at the University of California, Berkeley, was arrested by FBI agents at his cabin. On June 18 he was formally indicted on ten counts related to the transportation and mailing of explosive devices that killed or injured victims in California, New Jersey, and Connecticut. Supporting the government's case was evidence found in the Montana cabin and DNA evidence from saliva taken from letters linked to the Unabomber.

A variety of difficulties faced both the defense and prosecution in pretrial proceedings in *United States v. Kaczynski*. For instance, the defendant refused to cooperate with mental-health professionals during psychiatric exams, and Kaczynski also objected to undergoing neurological tests requested by his own lawyers. This refusal made it difficult for his defense team to pursue a diminished-capacity strategy. During these hearings, Kaczynski was frequently observed muttering to himself and, on one occasion, he threw a pen across the courtroom. In a surprising move, the judge ruled that Kaczynski could represent himself if he was proven competent by a court-appointed mental-health expert. Kaczynski then agreed to the mental health exam.

In January 1998, prior to opening statements, Kaczynski attempted suicide in jail and was placed under a 24-hour watch. In spite of the serious nature of his crimes, the prosecution was reluctant to seek the death penalty. Had Attorney General Janet Reno decided to seek the death penalty, the defense would have had solid ground for a constitutional challenge.

On January 22, 1998, Kaczynski accepted a plea bargain, entered an unconditional plea of guilty to all counts, and confessed to bombings for which he had not yet been formally charged. He was sentenced on May 4, 1998, to life in prison without the possibility of parole.

NBA Sees a Decade of Dominant Players

Jordan was not the only story in the NBA. Other great players were part of professional basketball and exhibited an "all-century" caliber. Magic Johnson and Larry Bird ended their illustrious careers in the early 1990s, and Tim Duncan began his career near the end of the decade. Charles Barkley, John Stockton, Shaquille O'Neal, David Robinson, Hakeem Olajuwon, Clyde Drexler, and Karl Malone all played magnificently. These players helped formed two Dream Teams to represent the United States during the 1992 and 1996 Olympics, and they crushed their opponents to win two gold medals. The league seemed to become more competitive in Jordan's absence when other "franchise" players had the opportunity to face-off.

Olajuwon, playing for the Houston Rockets, teamed with his former college teammate Clyde Drexler to defeat the Stockton-Malone duo of the Utah Jazz in an NBA Championship. Phoenix featured Barkley, while the San Antonio Spurs had league MVP Robinson. Orlando showcased the play of their star center O'Neal. Even with such talented players, professional basketball was usually a delight to behold when Jordan was on the court. In addition to the grace with which he played the game, he had the charisma to keep the public fascinated and tuned in.

Yet, none of the championship series in which the Bulls participated were blowouts. They always seemed vulnerable; there were enough subplots to keep the contests interesting and to make Jordan's heroics that much more amazing. In the 1996 finals against the Utah Jazz, Jordan faced Malone, who had won the MVP award that season. People wondered if the Malone-Stockton duo, after 11 years together, were good enough to overcome the Jordan-Pippen express. In the series Jordan averaged 36 points per game, hitting the buzzer-beater in the first game, scoring 38 points in the fifth game despite being ill, scoring another 39 points in the sixth and final game, and ultimately garnering MVP honors for the series.

It took all of Jordan's magic to overcome the bad feelings fans held toward professional basketball on other fronts. Latrell Sprewell's choking of his Golden State Warriors coach P.J. Carlesimo on December 1, 1997, and his threats to kill Carlesimo were considered by fans to be typical behavior of spoiled, rich athletes with whom spectators had little in common. It was impossible to retain the illusion that NBA stars were average men who had managed to succeed with hard work and talent. Clearly, such athletes were far from average. When a dispute between management and players threatened to halt play, it became difficult for fans to contemplate paying $400 to attend a game while billionaire owners and millionaire athletes demanded a greater share of the spoils.

123

Indie Films Find Mainstream Audiences

By the final decade of the twentieth century, "indie" movies were no longer just low-budget independently made films with unusual subject matter and reserved for small art-house theater. Instead, "indie" pictures constituted any film funded by sources other than a major studio, and some of the movies cost just as much to produce as studio-made movies.

Two critically-acclaimed independent movies of the 1990s were *Sling Blade* in 1996, which was written and directed by Billy Bob Thornton, who also starred in his own movie, and the 1996 *Fargo*, which was written by Joel and Ethan Coen and directed by Joel Coen. In *Sling Blade*, Thornton plays a mentally disabled man who murders someone out of good intentions. Roger Ebert said, "if *Forrest Gump* had been written by William Faulkner the result might have been something like *Sling Blade*." The movie was nominated for an Academy Award for Best Picture, and for his role in the movie, Thornton was nominated for the Best Actor in a Leading Role Academy Award. The film also earned Billy Bob Thornton an Oscar for Best Screenplay Adaptation. *Fargo*, a dark comedy that involved a winter kidnapping and murder in a small town, earned Frances McDormand an Academy Award for Best Actress and the Coens earned an Oscar for Best Screenplay.

Global Warming is Debated

During the 1990s, global warming became a major concern for scientists and the public. Many scientists warned that carbon dioxide and other gases from the burning of fossil fuels were collecting in the atmosphere and acting like the glass walls of a greenhouse, trapping heat on the surface of the Earth. They predicted that average temperatures could rise as much as 6.3 degrees F (3.5 degrees C) over the next century and threaten coastal areas with flooding as polar ice caps melted and warmer sea waters expanded, which, in their opinion, would ultimately lead to massive climate changes throughout the world. They cited evidence of heat waves, shrinking polar ice, and rising seas, all thought to be caused by global warming, and pointed to specific evidence that global warming was no longer a potential but a real threat to the environment. In Antarctica Adélie penguin populations declined 33 percent in 25 years because the sea ice where they lived was shrinking. In Bermuda and Hawaii rising seas killed coastal mangrove forests and caused beach erosion.

Skeptics questioned the presumed connection between human activity and global warming, arguing that while the global temperature might be rising, it could be the result of normal changes in weather patterns. They pointed out that Earth had undergone several major climate shifts throughout its known history and suggested that these normal shifts, not the burning of fossil fuels, were responsible for the changes in global temperature.

Scientific experiments and research, as well as international conferences throughout the decade, addressed concerns about global warming, and though the majority of climatologists accepted the premise that the burning of fossil fuels and the subsequent rise in carbon dioxide levels in the atmosphere was causing the planet to grow warmer, there was no consensus on how global warming might be reversed. Civilization had, since the 19th century, become too dependent on coal, oil, and natural gas to easily change its ways.

The 1996 Atlanta Summer Olympics Bombing and Competition

The Summer Olympics came to Atlanta in July 1996; the first time the games had been hosted by a city in the Southern United States. There was nothing typical about these Olympics. The very thing every host nation fears took place when tragedy struck and a homemade bomb exploded on July 27 in the Olympic Centennial Park, killing one woman (a cameraman died of a heart attack later) and injuring 111.

Following the precedent established by International Olympic Committee President Avery Brundage during the 1972 Olympics when 11 Israeli athletes were taken hostage and later murdered by terrorists, the games continued. His rationale, which probably preserved the future of the games, was that "We have only the strength of a great ideal. I am sure that the public would agree that we cannot allow a handful of terrorists to destroy this nucleus of international cooperation and goodwill we have in the Olympic movement. The Games must go on." Phillip Noel-Baker, an Olympian in 1912 and Nobel Peace Prize winner in 1959, agreed and concluded that sport may be humankind's "best hope."

In the competition venues, U.S. athletes shone, winning

44 gold medals, 32 silver, and 25 bronze. Russia was the nearest competitor at 26, 21, and 16 respectively. There was no lack of U.S. heroes during these games. Probably the most thrilling of all the competitors were the tiny members of the women's gymnastics team. Shannon Miller won the

gold with her prowess on the beam, and the team won the gold medal with a gutsy performance, especially that of 4'9" 18-year-old Kerri Strug, who made her last vault landing on a badly sprained ankle.

Michael Johnson, ignoring criticism that the track and field schedule had been specifically altered so that he could participate in both the 200- and 400-meter races, won both events. Gail Devers won her second-consecutive gold medal in the women's 100-meter race.

The American women's swim team dominated in the pool, winning seven of sixteen gold titles, along with five silvers and three bronzes. The men's swim team was not far behind with six golds, six silvers, and one bronze. The U.S. men's archery team was victorious, with Justin Huish winning the individual gold.

The Dream Team won in basketball. Andre Agassi and Lindsay Davenport won singles victories in tennis, and Gigi and Mary Jo Fernandez repeated as doubles champions. The U.S. women's soccer team won their event, a prelude to winning the World Cup in 1999—both victories gave women's athletics a boost in the United States unlike anything since Title IX of the Federal Education Amendments was enacted in 1972.

NASA Reveals Life on Mars

In 1996 NASA officials called a news conference to announce that a meteorite found in Antarctica in 1984 was discovered to contain organic compounds, minerals, and "carbon globules"—all of which indicated the presence of bacterial life on Mars. They also speculated that wormlike structures seen by electron microscopes could be the fossil remains of Martian microorganisms born billions of years ago when Mars was warmer and wetter. If the evidence was correctly interpreted, it could mean that life existed on Mars and might possibly be found on other planets as well. The announcement made banner headlines.

The evidence presented by NASA, however, came under attack from many experts. A UCLA specialist on ancient bacteria said it was unlikely that the findings proved bacterial life. In 1998, three papers on meteors were published suggesting that the same features were found in lunar meteorites and that the Mars meteorite was forged at temperatures too high for the formation of bacteria. Even NASA admitted that the evidence was not conclusive.

New York Yankees and Atlanta Braves Rule the Decade

A half-dozen different teams claimed World Series titles during the decade, despite the series game lost to the baseball strike. The New York Yankees won three championships (1996, 1998, and 1999); in 1998 they won more games (114) than any other team in baseball history. The Atlanta Braves also had a good decade, getting to the World Series five times, but winning only once in 1995.

The most unexpected championship season was provided by the Florida Marlins, the first and only team in major league history to win the World Series (1997) from a "wild card" berth. Immediately after the victory, owner Wayne Huizenga sold off the star players of his franchise, capitalizing on their high market value, and immediately watched his team drop from first to worst, from champs to last place in their division.

Tiger Woods Takes the PGA by Storm

Even in his 20s, Tiger Woods promised to become the best golfer who ever played the game. His performance at times was stellar; however, great golfers have to prove themselves over decades of play, and Woods had only just begun his professional career late in the 1990s. This early in his career, he was not yet capable of demonstrating the prowess of great golfers such as Jack Nicklaus and Ben Hogan. Nicklaus, after all, tied for sixth in the 1998 Masters at age 58, while Woods, in his golfing prime during the same tournament, tied for eighth. Still, what Woods did on the golf course was unprecedented and breathed far wider interest in a sport that was in danger of becoming staid.

Born Eldrick Tont Woods on December 30, 1975, to an African-American father and Thai mother, Woods's early years were the stuff of legend. He appeared on the Mike Douglas television show to demonstrate his golfing prowess at age two and was featured in Golf Digest at age five. He won Optimist International Junior

129

Tournaments six times (from age eight to fifteen). In an emotional speech, his father offered his "Tiger" as a gift to the world with portentous and ominous words, saying his son "will transcend this game and bring to the world humanitarianism, which has never been known before. The world will be a better place to live in by virtue of his existence and his presence." Whether or not there is truth to that claim, Woods was surely the consummate golfer.

Woods was the first player ever to win three consecutive U.S. Amateur Championships (1994-1996) and was also the NCAA Men's Individual Champion in 1996, playing for Stanford. As an amateur, he played impressively in the Grand Slam events, tying the British Open record for an amateur in 1996 as a 21-year-old. In the history of golf, the professional debut of no other player had ever been more anticipated than when Woods went pro on August 27, 1996.

In his 42nd week as a professional, at the age of 21 years and 24 weeks, he became the youngest player ever to be ranked the number-one golfer in the world by the Official World Ranking system. He also had the most rapid progression ever to achieve that ranking. He was the first player since 1990 to win two tour events in his first year as a pro and the first player since 1982 to record five straight top-five finishes. At the turn of the century, he topped that record by winning five consecutive tournaments. For sheer audacity, no feat compares with his victory at the Augusta National in 1997. With a record score of 270, 18 under par, Woods won by a record margin of 12 strokes. He was the first

African American and/or Asian American to win the contest, as well as the youngest golfer ever to win the Green Jacket.

By the end of the decade, Woods, who turned 24, had won 24 professional tournaments, 15 on PGA tour. In 1999 he was the first golfer to win four consecutive PGA events since Ben Hogan in 1953. He won another major championship in 1999, the PGA, and his tour earnings of $6,616,585 in the final year of the decade more than doubled the previous record total for one year.

His career earnings during the few years he played as a professional totaled $13,989,832, not including the millions paid to him for his endorsement contracts. Woods was selected by *Sports Illustrated* as the Sportsman of the Year in 1996, named the 1996 PGA Rookie of the Year, and was named both the Associated Press Male Athlete of the Year and PGA Tour Player of the Year in 1997 and 1999.

Lance Armstrong Survives Cancer and Wins Tour de France

Lance Armstrong was born September 18, 1971, in Plano, Texas. He started competing at an early age: he won the Iron Kids Triathlon at 13 and became a professional cyclist at age 16. Raised in a single-parent family by his mom, Linda, the young Texan achieved some significant athletic milestones before the age of 21. Even prior to his graduation from high school, Armstrong qualified to train with the U.S. Olympic developmental team. His first great cycling achievement was winning the U.S. National Amateur Championship in 1991. He competed in the 1992 Olympics in Barcelona as an amateur. His career continued to thrive, and in 1993 he won 10 titles, including the U.S. Pro Championship and World Champion, as well as one stage of the Tour de France. At the 1996 Olympics, Armstrong raced as a professional and was the highest-ranked cyclist in the world.

Armstrong then faced a foe more aggressive and deadlier than any he would ever meet on a cycling course. In October 1996 he was diagnosed with testicular cancer, which had spread to his lungs and brain. He was given a 50-50 chance of survival. Following surgeries to remove testicular and brain lesions, as well as undergoing aggressive chemotherapy treatments, Armstrong returned to training after only a five-month layoff. During his rehabilitation and return to cycling, Armstrong met and married fellow Texan Kristin Richard in May 1998. They had their first child in October 1999, Luke David Armstrong.

Not only was his personal life improving but so was his cycling. In 1998 Armstrong won the Sprint 56K Criterium in Austin, Tour de Luxembourg, Rhein-land-Pfalz Rundfarht in Germany, and the Cascade Classic in Oregon. The comeback, however, was not complete until Armstrong won the Tour de France on July 25, 1999, with a lead of 7 minutes and 38 seconds. Only one other non-European had ever won the prestigious event. Greg LeMond, also an American, was a three-time winner whose last victory was in 1990. LeMond was, however, supported by a European team, while

Armstrong used an American team sponsored by the U.S. Postal Service.

Mark Gorski, Armstrong's team manager, compared the victory to a contingent of French players winning the Super Bowl. According to Armstrong's agent, Bill Stapleton, the Tour de France victory would net Armstrong $2.5 million in prize money and bonuses from sponsors.

The 1996 Presidential Election

In the months after the disastrous 1994 election cycle in which Democrats lost numerous elections, it seemed unlikely that Clinton could sufficiently recover the political momentum necessary to secure a second term. Yet, he was once again the "Comeback Kid." He had learned from his 1980 gubernatorial re-election defeat and his comeback victory two years later, from the Gennifer Flowers extramarital affairs charge that almost destroyed his candidacy before he obtained the presidential nomination in 1992, and from the Republican success in capturing control of Congress in 1994, capitalizing on the lessons and turning them into a successful bid. His opponents for president in 1996 were Robert Joseph "Bob" Dole (R-Kansas) and H. Ross Perot (Reform Party). Clinton successfully mobilized his constituencies around the New Democratic agenda; he was also able to claim credit for a strong economy, welfare reform, and reduced crime. He won the 1996 election by a wider margin than in 1992, but it was still only a plurality of the votes cast. He received 49 percent of the popular vote, while Dole garnered 41 percent and Perot trailed with 8 percent.

20 RANDOM FACTS FROM 1996

1. On January 21, 1996, PLO chairman Yasser Arafat was elected the first president of Palestine in history.

2. On January 26, 1996, First Lady Hillary Rodham Clinton testified before a grand jury in regards to the Whitewater investigation.

3. On January 31, 1996, Tamil Tiger terrorists detonated a truck bomb in central Colombo, Sri Lanka, killing 55 and wounding 1,500.

4. On February 7, 1996, 189 people died when a Boeing 757 crashed off the coast of the Dominican Republic.

5. On February 9, 1996, an IRA bomb killed two in London, ending a 17-month ceasefire.

6. On February 25, 1996, two suicide bombers of Hamas, an Islamic extremist movement, killed 25 Israelis in Jerusalem and Ashkelon. In further attacks on March 3 and 4, thirty-four more were murdered.

7. On February 28, 1996, the 38th Grammy Awards presented Album of the Year for *Jagged Little Pill* by Alanis Morissette and Record of the Year for "Kiss From a Rose" by Seal.

8. On March 20, 1996, Lyle and Erik Menendez were sentenced to life in prison without parole for the

shotgun murders of their parents, Kitty and José Menendez.

9. On March 25, 1996, the 68th Academy Awards awarded *Braveheart* with Best Picture, Susan Sarandon as Best Actress for her role in *Dead Man Walking*, and Nicolas Cage as Best Actor for his role in *Leaving Las Vegas*.

10. On May 17, 1996, President Clinton signed into law an amendment to the 1994 Violent Crime Control and Law Enforcement Act. Known as Megan's Law, it requires the release of relevant information to protect the public from individuals convicted of sex offenses. The legislation was named after Megan Kanka, a murder victim of a convicted sex offender.

11. On May 21, 1996, 600 people died when an overloaded Tanzanian ferry sank on Lake Victoria.

12. On June 25, 1996, nineteen U.S. serviceman were killed in a terrorist bombing by Hezbollah-Gulf near Dhahran, Saudi Arabia.

13. On July 4, 1996, a bomb exploded on a crowded commuter train in Colombo, Sri Lanka, killing 70 people and injuring 450.

14. On July 17, 1996, the Federal Trade Commission (FTC) approved the Time-Warner merger with Turner Broadcasting System, creating the largest media company in the world.

15. On August 29, 1996, Russian government officials and Chechen rebel leaders signed a peace treaty,

ending nearly two years of fighting that resulted in 90,000 deaths.

16. On September 21, 1996, the Virginia Military Institute (VMI), a state-supported all-male military school, agreed to admit women.

17. On September 26, 1996, Israel declared a state of emergency after the worst fighting in 37 years occurred in the West Bank and Gaza Strip.

18. On November 11, 1996, a Saudi Arabian Boeing 747 collided with a Kazakh Airways Ilyushin-76 in midair, killing 340 people near Delhi, India.

19. In 1996 personal computer sales exceeded the sale of television sets for the first time.

20. On December 26, 1996, JonBenét Ramsey was found dead in her Boulder, Colorado, home. Her parents Patsy and John were suspects but no arrests were made.

TEST YOUR 1996 KNOWLEDGE
10 QUESTIONS

1) In which state was the Unabomber captured?

   a) Idaho
   b) Montana
   c) California

2) Which NBA basketball player choked his coach during practice?

   a) Latrell Sprewell
   b) Clyde Drexler
   c) Shaquille O'Neal

3) Which indie film released in the 1990s starred Billy Bob Thornton?

   a) *Fargo*
   b) *Pulp Fiction*
   c) *Sling Blade*

4) What did NASA claim to have discovered in 1996?

   a) Martian microorganisms
   b) New information about Neptune through the *Voyager 2* spacecraft
   c) Information about Jupiter through the *Galileo* spacecraft.

5) Which MLB team won three World Series titles in the 1990s?

   a) New York Yankees
   b) Atlanta Braves
   c) Florida Marlins

6) Which of the following did Tiger Woods accomplish in the 1990s?

   a) He won four consecutive PGA events
   b) He won the British Open
   c) He won the Masters at Augusta National twice

7) What almost ended Lance Armstrong's cycling career in the 1990s?

   a) A cycling crash
   b) Performance enhancing drugs
   c) Cancer

8) What was Bill Clinton's nickname in the 1990s?

   a) The Comeback Kid
   b) The Arkansas Adulterer
   c) The Arkansas Academic

9) Who was sentenced to life in prison for killing their parents in 1996?

   a) Lyle and Erik Menendez
   b) Alex and Derek King
   c) Jasmine Richardson and Jeremy Steinke

10) What does Megan's Law require?

   a) Inform the public about convicted sex offenders
   b) A five-day waiting period to purchase a handgun
   c) DNA testing for suspected sex offenders

ANSWERS

1) b

2) a

3) c

4) a

5) a

6) a

7) c

8) a

9) a

10) a

CHAPTER EIGHT
1997

MAJOR EVENTS

Pathfinder and Sojourner Land on Mars

On July 4, 1997, two unmanned spacecraft landed on Mars, the Mars Pathfinder and a rover stowed aboard it called Sojourner. The Mars Pathfinder, cushioned by large air bags, crash-landed on Mars and almost immediately began to send back dazzling images from the surface of the planet. Sojourner, the first autonomous vehicle to travel on another planet, rolled out onto the surface to sample soil and rocks. Pathfinder continued its work for three months, sending back 2.6 billion bits of information and 16,000 images.

Its last communication with Earth came on October 7; an effort to hail the spacecraft on November 1 was unsuccessful. The Mars Global Surveyor orbiter was also inserted into the Mars orbit in 1997 with the mission of circling the planet for two years to map its surface. NASA hoped that these maps would help locate suitable landing sites for future missions NASA planned to launch in 2001, 2003, and 2005.

Michael Jordan and the Chicago Bulls Dominate the NBA

Michael Jordan was possibly the best athlete in the history of basketball. Other players did not necessarily look bad in comparison to him, but they certainly fell under his enormous shadow. Opponents could occasionally block his shots, or, in a given game, score more points, but the 1990s was his decade. Even during the labor dispute of 1998-1999, the first work stoppage in the history of the NBA, Billy Hunter, executive director of the players association, needed Jordan's considerable influence on their side to ensure a favorable outcome for his constituency. Everyone understood that the game would not be the same when Jordan retired. It took no great marketing savvy to discern the significant difference in television ratings when Jordan and the Chicago Bulls were playing and when they were not. Jordan graciously delayed the announcement of his second retirement until the contract negotiations were concluded.

The Bulls, largely because of Jordan, were the dominant team of the decade, even leading the league in merchandise sales. Other great players were a part of the mix at various times, including Horace Grant, Scottie Pippen, and Dennis Rodman. They also had an impressive coach in Phil Jackson. How these talented men might have succeeded without Jordan will never be known. For example, throughout the decade Jackson won six titles as Jordan's coach but none without him.

Mike Tyson Bites an Ear and Professional Boxing Stumbles

The sport of boxing, never tidy, was complicated and confusing during the 1990s. Much of what was not mystifying—for example, Mike Tyson biting off part of Evander Holyfield's ear during a 1997 bout—was deplorable. People began to compare professional boxing with professional wrestling, an image not helped when Tyson agreed to "referee" a wrestling match in Boston. The state of Washington broke another precedent when it sanctioned a boxing match between a man and woman—she won.

It was a decade in which even boxing enthusiasts had a hard time finding positive things to say about their sport. Richard Hoffer, of *Sports Illustrated*, complained of the "forgettable seasons in boxing" and "unearned dollars for unexciting fights." In a fit of editorial pique, Hoffer wrote, "Holyfield zipped up to New York to meet Akinwande who had earned this title shot by, well, no one could say how." Tim Graham, writing for ESPN.com, argued that the final year of the decade with regard to boxing was "an all-time low. Rather than glory, the year was rife with larceny, tragedy, gluttony, stupidity. They're all ingrained aspects of the sport, but such heavy doses of them all were enough to choke a goat."

Part of the problem in 1999 was related to the indictments of International Boxing Federation (IBF) president Robert W. Lee Sr. and three others for accepting bribes and soliciting payments to alter rankings and arrange fights. It was hardly a decade to inspire confidence in fans of boxing.

The Metal Revival and Marilyn Manson

Heavy metal experienced a revival at the end of the 1990s, after dominating the beginning of the decade and losing ground in the middle. In 1997 the first Ozzfest, featuring Marilyn Manson, grossed nearly as much money as the highest grossing women's rock tour, the Lilith Fair. The metal bands of the 1990s were aggressive with disturbing lyrics and heavy guitars with influences from hip-hop and electronic music.

The band Marilyn Manson used neo-Satanism as a gimmick to attract controversy and audiences. Their millions of fans loved their heavy sound and occult mystique. The band originated in 1989 when singer and songwriter Brian Warner met guitarist Scott Putesky; Warner assumed the stage name Marilyn Manson, which blended the names of movie star Marilyn Monroe and convicted murderer Charles Manson, and Putesky became Daisy Berkowitz, a combination of Daisy Duke from the show *Dukes of Hazard* and serial killer David Berkowitz. Eventually, they added new band members to form Marilyn Manson and the Spooky Kids, but changed the name in 1992 to just Marilyn Manson.

The following year, Trent Reznor of Nine Inch Nails signed the band to a recording contract on his Nothing Records label, and Marilyn Manson began opening shows for Nine Inch Nails. Marilyn Manson's first album *Portrait of an American Family* was released in July 1994, and their exposure during Nine Inch Nails concerts helped them gain a legion of metal fans.

From there, Marilyn Manson set out to purposely offend religious organizations as a means to publicize the band, and Warner even became an honorary minister in the Church of Satan. During a show in Utah, he tore up a copy of the Book of Mormon, and the group's 1996 album *Antichrist Superstar* did nothing to ease worries of conservatives about its Satanism. In October 1996 the recording reached number three on the Billboard albums chart and sold 1.4 million copies, and the radio began to play their single "The Beautiful People."

Pat Robertson's 700 Club protested Marilyn Manson concerts and managed to get some of their shows canceled, but religious protest only increased their popularity. In the late 1990s Manson turned to "glam rock," which included elaborate costumes and stage sets.

Oklahoma City Bomber is Sentenced to Death

Exactly two years after the assault on the Mt. Carmel compound in Waco, a homemade bomb that an American terrorist hid in a rented truck exploded at the Alfred P. Murrah Federal Building in Oklahoma City, Oklahoma. The assault on the building and the workforce inside killed 168 individuals, which included 19 children under the age of five. The Murrah Building was the home of a variety of federal agencies, as well as a daycare center for the children of those federal employees. The motive behind the most-deadly domestic terrorist attack in American history was antigovernment sentiment related to the raid on the Branch Davidians, which had a disastrous conclusion.

Ninety minutes after the explosion, Timothy James McVeigh was arrested on an unrelated weapons violation during a routine traffic stop. On April 21, 1995, McVeigh, a U.S. Army combat veteran who was awarded the Bronze Star for his service in the Gulf War, was charged by federal authorities in connection with the bombing. Terry Lynn Nichols, also a former soldier, was charged as his accomplice on May 10, 1995, and on August 11, a grand jury indicted McVeigh and Nichols for murder and the use of a weapon of mass destruction. Federal prosecutors sought the death penalty in both cases.

Opening statements began on April 24, 1997. The federal prosecution team focused the case against McVeigh on the evidence that he rented a Ryder truck and used it to carry the ammonium-nitrate bomb. Prosecutors also proved that McVeigh's fingerprints were on a receipt for the purchase of 45-pound bags of fertilizer used in the bombing. Government prosecutors also showed that McVeigh's clothing was covered with bomb residue when he was arrested.

McVeigh's defense attempted to foster reasonable doubt in the minds of the jurors by focusing on the circumstantial nature of the evidence collected and criticized the competency of FBI crime lab procedures. The defense also contended that McVeigh was not the bomber, and that another person who had accompanied McVeigh to rent the Ryder vehicle was the one who carried out the bombing. McVeigh did not testify, and on June 2, 1997, a jury convicted him on all charges, and he was sentenced to death by lethal injection. Nichols was tried separately from McVeigh, and in the end, he was sentenced to life in prison without the possibility of parole.

New Age Spirituality and a Christianized America

Americans might have been concerned with cyberspace in the 1990s, but they were also preoccupied with "inner space." In the quest to discover richer spiritual lives, they began returning to mainstream churches but also looked to spiritual alternatives. New Age spirituality prospered during the 1990s with the help of New Age gurus like Deepak Chopra.

The phenomenon of corporate spiritualism transformed the culture of offices in many companies and became popular as a means to motivate employees by emphasizing individual autonomy, obligations to the company as well as to God, and a personal responsibility to find happiness and fulfillment. Evangelical Christian entrepreneurs worked hard to Christianize American society through their business and commerce, and these Christian capitalists believed that religion belonged in the workplace and was essential to financial success. They regarded themselves as spiritual and economic leaders who were engaged in a covenant with God and in a custodial relationship outside of their homes with their employees and customers.

Recycling is Taken More Seriously

In the 1990s Americans threw away more than 430 billion pounds of garbage each year, and U.S. industries unloaded 2.5 billion pounds of toxic waste per year. Finding new ways to decrease waste and recycle garbage became a great concern, and by the end of the decade, eco-industrial parks in which numerous companies shared resources were being developed around the world. Furthermore, biotechnology was finding new tools to deal with waste. For instance, it was discovered that certain microbes were capable of converting toxic substances in contaminated soil or sludge into harmless byproducts. In the consumer market, emphasis on recycling led to trends such as designing and making clothes from used plastic bottles, briefcases from worn-out tires, and belts from beer-bottle caps.

By 1999, 25 percent of the 430 billion pounds of U.S. garbage was being recycled, and experts believed that the number would increase as industries developed materials that could more easily be reused and if manufacturers created products with thinner aluminum and plastic containers.

Martha Stewart Becomes the Last Word on Décor and Cooking

Teaching people how to create an elegant dessert or make their Christmas wreath may have been enough for Martha Stewart in the 1980s, but in the 1990s Stewart set out to conquer the world. In 1997 she aligned herself in a newly revised business partnership with the discount retailer K-Mart and unveiled a series of products from sheets to paint in order to increase the sales and profits of both K-Mart and herself.

She weighed in on issues from dyeing Easter eggs to collecting glass in her "askMartha" newspaper column that reached an estimated 80 million readers a month, and she launched a new web business that combined the sales of domestic merchandise and how-to advice. She also acquired her own television show, published the magazine "Martha Living," and unveiled "Martha" as a stock entity when shares of Martha Stewart Living Omnimedia Inc. went public in October 1999. When K-Mart officials learned that more people trusted Stewart than their own doctors, they wasted no time in proposing a partnership that netted Stewart a sizable profit up front and guaranteed her a percentage of every "Martha Item" that K-Mart sold.

Cyber Attack Vulnerability and a Hacker Makes the FBI's Most Wanted List

In 1997 Congress spent $3 billion to upgrade the U.S. military's defense system against information warfare. The United States was the most computer-dependent nation in the world, making it uniquely vulnerable to cyber attacks, and the Pentagon believed that outsiders probed U.S. military computers close to a thousand times per day. These hackers ranged from malicious governments and citizens to curious and naïve teenagers.

In August 1999 Attorney General Janet Reno established the Internet Working Group to address the issue of cyber crime. The group found that the Internet presented new and significant challenges for law enforcement at all levels, and the Group issued a report called "The Electronic Frontier: The Challenge of Unlawful Conduct Involving the Use of the Internet," which recommended new investigative tools, increased training for law enforcement officials, and more legal authority over the Internet.

The ACLU, however, found fault with the report and argued that the report contained dangerous recommendations that stripped away privacy, free speech, and free press protection, and the ACLU argued that anonymity, even on the Internet, was a basic constitutional right.

The case of Kevin Mitnick highlighted the dilemmas that hackers brought to the American legal system. On January 21, 2000, Mitnick was released from prison after serving a five-year sentence for charges of computer and wire fraud. He became an underground celebrity after leading the FBI on a three-year manhunt that ended in 1995 when investigators finally traced his electronic signals to an apartment in Raleigh, North Carolina. He was the only computer hacker to make the FBI's most wanted list.

Mitnick, who began hacking when he was a teenager, was accused of causing millions of dollars of damage by hacking into the computers of such companies as Motorola, Novell, Nokia, and Sun Microsystems, as well as the University of California, and stealing software, product plans, and other data. Mitnick was sentenced to five years in prison in March 1999 after pleading guilty to five felony counts. He was given credit for four years served while awaiting trial.

In a case that highlighted the new challenges that Internet technology and security brought to the courts, Mitnick spent four years in jail after his arrest, awaiting sentencing because high-tech crimes were often too complex for police and prosecutors to handle, a fact that led to unnecessary searches, arrests, and court delays. Often, the only person able to understand and explain the technical details of the alleged crime was the defendant. Lack of technical expertise by the prosecutors and a lack of precedents in the courts contributed to delays.

During the 1990s, between 64 percent and 78 percent of federal computer-fraud cases were tossed out or sent to the states for prosecution. While government agencies tried to strengthen laws against cyber crimes and tighten national defenses, many civil rights groups argued that new laws violated individual and corporate privacy and enforced rules that were unnecessary. Some feared a threat to the decentralized, inclusive nature of the Internet if government agencies were allowed to monitor anyone's activity while in cyberspace. Another problem with prosecuting hackers was determining accurately what damages and costs had actually been incurred.

In Mitnick's case, corporations were asked by the prosecutors to show the total amount of investment that went into the items allegedly stolen. Sun Microsystems claimed that the source code Mitnick allegedly stole was worth $80 million, even though Sun later sold copies of that same code to students and software developers for $100 each. Mitnick's lawyer argued that

151

a distinction should be made between a recreational hacker and a thief or terrorist because Mitnick did not destroy or erase the codes he accessed.

After his release, Mitnick read a statement claiming that his crimes were exaggerated and that the prosecution and media hindered his ability to present a legal defense. He said his crimes were simply trespassing out of curiosity. He claimed he did it for fun, not for profit. In a strange twist, as the decade closed, he advised a Senate panel on ways that hackers could infiltrate sensitive computer systems and ways those systems could be made more secure. Mitnick counseled the panel to require agencies to assess what data is most important and to train employees to recognize an attack in progress.

Harry Potter Becomes a Phenomenon

Throughout the latter part of the decade, thousands of children walked around with paste-on tattoos in the shape of a purple lightning bolt. Many adults were puzzled, but for those in the know, the tattoos indicated that these kids were fans of a young wizard named Harry Potter. The fictional character and his adventures were the creation of English author J.K. Rowling, and Potter's tales captivated readers of all ages. Three books, *Harry Potter and the Sorcerer's Stone* in 1998, *Harry Potter and the Chamber of Secrets* in 1999, and *Harry Potter and the Prisoner of Azkaban* in 1999, racked up record-breaking sales in the United Kingdom and the United States.

The books also earned the distinction as one of the few children's books ever to break into the adult best-sellers list, remaining on *The New York Times* Best Sellers list for more than 38 weeks. By the fall of 1999, more than 7.5 million volumes were in print, and it had been translated into 28 languages, resulting in more than 650,000 lightning-bolt tattoos having been sold at bookstores across the country.

20 RANDOM FACTS FROM 1997

1. On January 15, 1997, Israeli and Palestinian cabinets approved a new peace arrangement concerning Hebron, in which 80 percent of the West Bank would be placed under Palestinian Control.

2. On February 4, 1997, 73 Israeli servicemen are killed when two helicopters crashed near the border of southern Lebanon.

3. On February 12, 1997, an Iranian-sponsored foundation increased the bounty for killing Salman Rushdie, author of *The Satanic Verses* released in 1989, to $2.5 million. The book is deemed as blasphemous to Muslims.

4. On February 26, 1997, the 39th Grammy Awards award Album of the Year for *Falling Into You* by Celine Dion and "Change the World" by Eric Clapton as the Record of the Year.

5. On March 13, 1997, a Jordanian soldier shot and killed seven Israeli schoolgirls at the Hill of Peace in the Jordan Valley.

6. On March 24, 1997, the 69th Academy Awards presented Best Picture for *The English Patient*, Best Actress to Francis McDormand for her role in *Fargo*, and Best Actor to Geoffrey Rush for his role in *Shine*.

7. In March 1997 the Hale-Bopp comet soared close to Earth (122 million miles).

8. On May 2, 1997, Tony Blair was appointed the youngest prime minister in Britain since 1812. The 43-year-old won by a landslide victory.

9. On May 10, 1997, an earthquake in Iran, near the Afghan border, resulted in the death of 1,600 people.

10. On May 11, 1997, the IBM supercomputer Deep Blue made chess history by defeating Gary Kasparov, the first time a reigning world champion was beaten in a match by a machine.

11. On May 17, 1997, after 32 years in power, President Mobutu of Zaire fled to Morocco. Rebel leader Laurent Kabila proclaimed himself head of state and renamed the country the Democratic Republic of Congo.

12. On June 30, 1997, the city of Hong Kong returned to Chinese sovereignty after 156 years as a British colony.

13. On July 4, 1997, the U.S. Pathfinder space probe, carrying the Sojourner rover, made an historic landing on Mars.

14. On August 5, 1997, a Korean Boeing 747 crashed in Guam, killing 220 people.

15. On August 31, 1997, the Princess of Wales died in a car crash in Paris. An estimated two billion people watched her funeral in London on September 6.

16. On September 5, 1997, Mother Theresa died from heart failure, and dignitaries from around the world attended her funeral on September 13.

17. On September 25, 1997, Briton Andy Green set a new world land-speed record of 714 mph when he drove the jet-powered car Thrust SSC across the Nevada desert. On October 17 he became the first person to break the sound barrier on land, reaching a speed of 764.18 mph.

18. On October 8, 1997, Kim Jong Il, son of the late Kim Il Sung, became the general secretary of the ruling Worker's Party in North Korea.

19. On October 9, 1997, Hurricane Pauline struck the Pacific resort of Acapulco, killing 400 people.

20. In 1997 U.S. farmers planted genetically modified soy on more than 8 million acres and genetically modified corn on more than 3.5 million acres.

TEST YOUR 1997 KNOWLEDGE
10 QUESTIONS

1) What was the name of the NASA rover that traveled over the face of Mars in the 1990s?

   a) Pathfinder
   b) Sojourner
   c) Spirit

2) Which professional boxer bit his opponent's ear in 1997?

   a) Evander Holyfield
   b) Mike Tyson
   c) Lennox Lewis

3) Which book did singer Marilyn Manson rip to pieces during a concert?

   a) The Koran
   b) The Book of Mormon
   c) The Holy Bible

4) Which building did Timothy McVeigh target?

   a) Alfred P. Murrah Federal Building
   b) The World Trade Center
   c) The Branch Davidian Complex

5) Which company joined forces with Martha Stewart in the 1990s?

   a) Target
   b) Sears
   c) K-Mart

6) Which book series inspired kids to buy millions of books in the late 1990s?

   a) Lord of the Rings
   b) Harry Potter
   c) A Game of Thrones

7) Which author had a death bounty placed on him for a book he wrote?

   a) Salman Rushdie
   b) John Grisham
   c) Brett Easton Ellis

8) Who was appointed the youngest prime minister in Britain since 1812?

   a) Tony Blair
   b) John Major
   c) Gordon Brown

9) Which Asian territory did Britain return after 156 years as a British colony?

   a) Taiwan
   b) Hong Kong
   c) Singapore

10) Which charitable woman died due to heart complications in 1997?

   a) Princess Diana
   b) Mother Theresa
   c) Gail Davis

ANSWERS

1) b

2) b

3) b

4) a

5) c

6) b

7) a

8) a

9) b

10) b

CHAPTER NINE
1998

MAJOR EVENTS

The 1998 Nagano Winter Olympics

From a U.S. point of view, the notable thing about the 1998 Winter Olympics was the 14-hour time difference between the eastern coast time zone of America and Nagano, Japan. It was nearly impossible for CBS to maintain suspense about events when cable news channels announced the winners as the events were completed. By the time CBS showed a recording of ski racer Picabo Street's gold-medal run in the women's Alpine super G, the result had already been announced by CNN and ESPN, and she had already been interviewed by network morning shows.

The U.S. team won six gold medals that included three in the new "extreme" events of freestyle skiing. Professional hockey players were allowed in the competition for the first time, and the U.S. hockey team disappointed Americans by their actions both on and off the ice. They lost an important match to the Czech Republic then trashed three Olympic apartments in a display of sour sportsmanship. The U.S. women's hockey team stepped up to redeem the sport for Americans by winning the gold, and a wonderful surprise was the gold-medal performance of 16-year-old figure skater Tara Lipinski.

Increase in Road Rage Incidents

In the 1990s American drivers became more dangerous than ever before. By 1998, road rage incidents in which an angry driver hurt or killed another driver rose by 51 percent from the start of the decade, and 37 percent of drivers involved in aggressive driving incidents used a firearm against other drivers, 28 percent used other weapon types, and 35 percent used their vehicles.

Road rage became such an issue that Congress discussed ways to punish offenders, and psychologists said that aggressive driving had become normal for drivers, creating a subculture of Americans. Heavy traffic, long commutes, and bigger vehicles have created dangerous behavior through shorter tempers.

The Cellular Phone Becomes a Staple

The hot new device for many Americans during the 1990s was the cell phone. Since the early 1980s, cellular service had been available, but the 1990s brought cheaper phones and affordable service, which created higher demand. By 1998, 63 million Americans had some type of cell phone service.

With the rise of mobile use, society had to confront many issues involving phone etiquette, and many debated the use of cellular phones while driving. The *New England Journal of Medicine* reported that people talking on a phone while driving were four times more likely to cause an accident, putting them in the same category as drunk drivers.

Generation X

Overshadowed by the 78 million Baby Boomers, the 45 million people born between 1965 and 1984 still made a lot of noise during the 1990s. Known as "Generation X," the generation was considered cynical, lazy, and unfocused by the older generation, but the portrayal was unfair. Unlike Baby Boomers who grow up mostly in affluent circumstances and came to accept prosperity as their due, Generation X presumed nothing. They grew up during a 1980's recession; lived through increased divorce rates, the AIDS epidemic, and the Cold War; and entered a tight workforce with few rewards. Despite the hurdles, "Gen Xers" showed themselves to be full of ambition, technologically knowledgeable—having been the first generation to grow up with personal computers—hardworking, and self-assured. Dedicated to social causes and global concerns, they found unique ways to make money and represented $125 billion in purchasing power a year.

The Growing Popularity of the SUV

In America the preferred vehicle of the 1990s was the Sports Utility Vehicle (SUV). From 1990 to 1998, sales of SUVs doubled, and more than three million were sold in 1998 alone. The vehicle offered drivers lots of room for passengers, families, and cargo; and like vans and trucks, they sat higher off the ground, making it easier for drivers to see traffic. By 1998 there were more than 40 different SUV models, including offerings from Ford (manufacturer of the most popular model in the Ford Explorer), Jeep, Chevrolet, GMC,

Nissan, and Toyota. Even luxury-car manufacturers such as Mercedes Benz and Lexus offered a luxury SUV for the discriminating driver.

The MP3 Opens a New Frontier and Brings Fear

The MP3 was a computer format that compressed CD-quality audio files into only a few megabytes, making high-quality audio easy to digitally download. The format concerned music industry executives because it was often downloaded illegally, which they called theft of intellectual property. Numerous websites popped up that did not obtain copyright permissions but offered access to songs for free or unmonitored trading, which posed a threat to the sales and royalty income for both record labels and performers.

While record companies took measures in 1998 and 1999 to bring bootlegging under control, some recording artists believed the MP3 format was a good thing because it introduced a new way to bring their music to the people. With the introduction of portable MP3 devices in 1998, the MP3 became the most popular offering in audio. The early gadgets held around 60 minutes of music, and benefits for users included options to change out the music files whenever they wished and to arrange the music into playlists. In 1998 record companies sued portable MP3 player manufactures in an attempt to keep them off the market, but they lost their case.

MLB's Mark McGwire and Sammy Sosa Put on Show

The great homerun battle of 1998 starred Sammy Sosa of the Chicago Cubs and Mark McGwire of the St. Louis Cardinals, who both hit more homeruns in a season than any other person in MLB history as they lit up National League scoreboards. More importantly, McGwire and Sosa gifted MLB with immeasurable amounts of goodwill after a season of strikes by the players ended in the cancellation of the World Series.

Roger Maris's 61 homeruns in 1961was considered the most-revered record in baseball, and no one had come close to breaking it for three decades. Many experts thought that Maris's record was a fluke, one that no player could ever break, but then 1998 arrived with variables never before witnessed in MLB. The league expanded into two new markets in the span of a single year, Tampa Bay and Arizona, which diluted the quality of pitching in the league, and with long-ball friendly Coors Field in Colorado in play as well, the stage was set for an unequalled homerun derby.

First Sosa set a major league record in June 1998 when he hit 20 homeruns, the most ever by a player in a single month. Additionally, his 11 multiple-homerun games tied the major league record. He also led the majors in RBIs and total bases, and at the end of the season earned MVP of the National League. During this season, Sosa hit 66 homeruns, which was more than any other player, except McGwire, who slammed baseballs out of the park 70 times.

New MLB Ballparks are Built in Numerous Markets

Many people claimed that 1998 was the greatest MLB season to ever be played, and a full recovery was in bloom after a devastating strike led to the cancellation of a World Series. Baseball, considered America's national pastime, had righted itself by the end of the decade through the goodwill of its players, and the 1990s brought a return to ballpark architecture and fiscal sanity. Rather than the generic and symmetrical stadiums of the 1960s and 1970s, the opening of Camden Yards in 1992 spurred a decade of interesting, varied, fan-friendly parks for baseball consumption. Other glorious parks appeared in the 1990s: The Ballpark (1994) located within Globe Life Park in Arlington, Texas, the home of the Rangers; Turner Field (1997) in Georgia, the home of the Braves; the first stadium built with a retractable-domed ballpark at Chase Field (1998) in Phoenix, the home of the Arizona Diamondbacks; and Jacobs Field (1994), the home of the Cleveland Indians.

Primetime Cartoon for Adults

At the end of the decade, what was the longest-running situation comedy in primetime? *The Simpsons*. With the success of this show, television executives learned that cartoons were not just for kids on Saturday morning. By the end of the 1990s, FOX, MTV, and WB were all running primetime cartoons. While *The Simpsons* was by far the most consistently excellent animated series, several other shows provided primetime laughs and acquired devoted followings.

In 1994 *The Simpsons* became the first regular primetime series to be simulcast in Spanish, and in February 1997 it became the longest-running cartoon on primetime, surpassing the record set by *The Flintstones* from 1960-1966. Other favorites included *Beavis & Butt-Head*, which debuted in 1993, *King of the Hill*, which debuted after Super Bowl XXXI on January 12, 1997, *Futurama*, which debuted March 3, 1999, *Family Guy*, which debuted on April 6, 1999, *Daria*, which premiered on March 3, 1997, and *The PJ's*, which debuted in January 1999.

The International Space Station Takes Form

The International Space Station (ISS) was a cooperative project involving the United States, Russia, Japan, Canada, and 11 members of the European Space Agency. It was billed as a "city in space," and conceived by NASA in 1983, but it wasn't until November 20, 1998, that a Russian Proton rocket blasted off from the Baikonur Cosmodrome in Kazakhstan, carrying the first piece of the station. A month later, the U.S. *Space Shuttle Endeavour* brought the second piece, a connecting module called Node 1, or Unity.

At the end of the 1990s, the program was awaiting the launch of the Russian service module Zvezda, which could potentially provide the temporary living space of hundreds of astronauts over the life of the station. The station would eventually become the size of a football field and weigh 520 tons, and ultimately serve as a platform for space research and scientific experimentation. The key source of energy for the station would be solar panels.

20 RANDOM FACTS FROM 1998

1. On January 4, 1998, Amnesty International reported that more than 80,000 people had died as a result of fighting in Algeria since 1992.

2. On January 25, 1998, Tamil Tigers bombed Sri Lanka's holiest shrine, the Temple of the Tooth, in Kandy, killing 11.

3. On February 3, 1998, a U.S. military aircraft accidentally severed the suspension wire of a cable car at an Italian ski resort, which resulted in the death of 20 people.

4. On February 4, 1998, an earthquake in northern Afghanistan killed 4,000 people.

5. On February 16, 1998, a Taiwanese A-300 Airbus crashed on approach to Taipei and 260 people were killed.

6. On February 23, 1998, UN Secretary-General Kofi Annan and Iraqi leaders reached an agreement to allow UN weapons inspectors unrestricted access to all sites in Iraq.

7. On February 25, 1998, the 40th Grammy Awards awarded *Time Out of Mind* by Bob Dylan as Album of the Year and "Sunny Came Home" by Shawn Colvin as the Record of the Year.

8. On March 23, 1998, the 70th Academy Awards awarded *Titanic* as Best Picture, Helen Hunt as

Best Actress for her role in *As Good as It Gets*, and Jack Nicholson as Best Actor for his role alongside Helen Hunt.

9. On April 15, 1998, Pol Pot, the former Khmer Rouge dictator of Cambodia, died.

10. On April 24, 1998, 22 men and women were publicly executed in Rwanda for their part in the 1994 massacres.

11. On May 30, 1998, the second earthquake to hit in Northern Afghanistan in 1998 killed 3,000 people.

12. On June 13, 1998, Queen Margrethe II of Denmark opened the four-mile long Storebælt Bridge, linking Eastern and Western Denmark. It is the second longest suspension bridge in the world.

13. On June 16, 1998, a cyclone hit northern India, leaving 1,300 dead and 10,000 missing.

14. On July 17, 1998, a massive tsunami tidal wave hit the northwestern coast of Papua New Guinea, killing 3,000 people.

15. On August 7, 1998, a car bomb exploded outside the U.S. embassy in Nairobi, Kenya, killing 240 people and injuring 5,000. Another terrorist bomb in Dar es Salaam, Tanzania, killed 10.

16. On August 17, 1998, President Clinton testified before a grand jury and admitted his affair with Monica Lewinsky.

17. On August 20, 1998, the United States launched cruise missiles at suspected terrorist bases in

Afghanistan and at a chemical weapons facility in Sudan in retaliation for the August 7 attacks on embassies in East Africa.

18. On December 19, 1998, the House of Representatives approved two articles of impeachment against President Clinton.

19. In November 1998 two research teams succeeded in growing embryonic stem cells.

20. In 1998 software maker Microsoft surpassed General Electric as the biggest company in the United States.

TEST YOUR 1998 KNOWLEDGE
10 QUESTIONS

1) Who won the gold medal in figure skating in the 1998 Winter Olympics?

   a) Tara Lipinski
   b) Tonya Harding
   c) Nancy Kerrigan

2) Who hit the most homeruns during the 1998 MLB season, shattering the previous record?

   a) Sammy Sosa
   b) Mark McGwire
   c) Ken Griffey Jr.

3) Which 1990s show became the longest-running primetime cartoon?

   a) *King of the Hill*
   b) *Family Guy*
   c) *The Simpsons*

4) Where did a military aircraft cut a cable car suspension wire, killing 20 people?

   a) Norway
   b) Sweden
   c) Italy

5) Which film won the 70th Academy Award for Best Picture in 1998?

   a) *As Good as it Gets*

b) *Saving Private Ryan*
c) *Titanic*

6) What country was struck by a tsunami tidal wave in 1998, killing more than 3,000 people?

a) Papua New Guinea
b) Haiti
c) Puerto Rico

7) In 1997, which company passed General Electric as the biggest in the United States?

a) Wal-Mart
b) American Online
c) Microsoft

8) What was billed as a "city in space?"

a) Mir Space station
b) International Space Station
c) Biosphere 2

9) What technical gadget created fear in the recording industry in the late 1990s?

a) Digital recording devices
b) MP3 player
c) Mobile phones

10) Which type of vehicle became popular in the 1990s?

a) SUV
b) Station wagon
c) Smart car

ANSWERS

1) a
2) b
3) c
4) c
5) c
6) a
7) c
8) b
9) b
10) a

CHAPTER TEN
1999

MAJOR EVENTS

A Revolution Without Borders but with Multilateral Cooperation

The 1990s was a decade of transition, from a Cold War struggle between two powerful countries based on political ideology and nationalism to technological and economic competition between businesses and financial institutions that had little concern about borders. This new development forced leaders to change the way they conducted themselves or fall behind; still, many stubbornly refused to do so. The United States began the decade as the only superpower, and it found its strength by tapping into a technological and economic revolution that had no borders

The second major transition during the 1990s was the way in which the world governed itself. Instead of isolation and nationalism, countries embraced a new ideology of multilateral cooperation to resolve international problems. The Gulf War in 1991 strengthened the notion that a multilateral approach to conflict through the United Nations was a surefire approach to quick resolutions. However, too often, the coalition was slow to act when it came to ethnic conflicts in Indonesia, Rwanda, Indonesia, the former Yugoslavia, and the independent states of the former Soviet Union.

Teen Violence and Columbine

The 1990s saw a disturbing trend of growing youth violence in the United States. Serious crimes committed by juveniles skyrocketed at the beginning of the decade, reaching new high rates, which led to a message of high alert being sent to the masses on April 20, 1999, when two students fired high-powered weapons through the halls and classrooms of a suburban high school in Littleton, Colorado. Students Eric Harris, 18, and Dylan Klebold, 17, killed 15 people and injured 20 others before killing themselves.

The Columbine High School massacre was only one of numerous school shootings during the decade. On February 2, 1996, a student walked into his algebra class in Moses Lake, Washington, and killed his teacher and two students. On February 19, 1997, in Bethel, Alaska, a student killed the principal and a student. On October 1, 1997, a student stabbed his mother to death in Pearl, Mississippi, and then shot and killed two classmates. On December 1, 1997, in West Paducah, Kentucky, three students were killed; then in 1998 a student murdered a teacher in Edinboro, Pennsylvania; four students and a teacher were killed in Jonesboro, Arkansas; and in Springfield, Oregon, a student killed his parents and two students.

Because of suburban school shootings, administrators increased security measures by hiring security, requiring see-through backpacks, installing metal detectors, and routinely checking student lockers. Furthermore, many schools instituted a "zero-tolerance" policy for violence and implemented programs designed to help students with behavioral problems. In an attempt to find answers to why suburban kids from stable, middle class homes would resort to violence, some blamed violent movies and television shows, the Internet, video games, and music.

The Resurrection of Ethnic Conflicts

In many ways, the irony of the end of the Cold War was that it made the world safe for a resurrection of ethnic conflicts. Although there were some efforts to moderate these clashes in Kosovo and Bosnia, in many cases, multilateral efforts were too slow to act, or completely refused to intervene, which was the case in Rwanda, East Timor, and Chechnya.

The difficulties in the ongoing peace process between Israel and its neighbors, including the Palestinians, were about land rights. Similarly, ethnic conflicts in central Africa and the former Yugoslavia arose from a repetitive cycle of oppression and killing, ongoing animosity, and land claims.

The media and international conferences discussed human rights issues at length at, but no one could decide upon a clear definition of "human rights" what constituted "abuse," or what solutions might work, and many died in the waiting.

Globalization Becomes the New World Economy

Old land claims and animosities impeded globalization, and the global system bypassed nations that insisted on maintaining their ancient ways. The world was integrating in the 1990s, and those integrations included markets, technologies, and entire countries. It was simple. Populaces that accepted free-market capitalism had economic stability and growth, and those that failed to do so suffered through poverty, instability, and violence. The last years of the decade were a struggle for nations that were not clear where they stood, even though it was obvious that the countries that were experiencing prosperity had joined the global system.

Latin and Pop Crossover

The biggest reason for a renewed popularity of Latin music during the 1990s was Ricky Martin, who impressed attendees at the 1999 Grammy Awards with his hip-hop rendition of "The Cup of Life." Formerly a teen vocalist in the 1980s group Menudo, Martin made the most of his Latin looks and vocal abilities during the late 1990s. His album *Ricky Martin* rose to number one on the album charts in May 1999, and in August he told *Rolling Stone* "I said, 'Wait a minute. Keep it simple. You were born in Puerto Rico, and you're a Latin—even though the first stuff you listened to was Journey, Foreigner, Cheap Trick, Boston—so let's play with it a little, not be stereotypical. '"

Jennifer Lopez was another popular musician during the Latin pop music movement. She got her start as the star of *Selena* in 1997, a film about a young Mexican singer. Lopez's dance moves and singing ability served her well in the recording business. May 4, 1999, was the release date of her debut single "If You Had My Love" that made the Billboard Hot 100.

Another popular song that combined Afro-Cuban and Latin-style music rhythms, known as mambo, hit the charts in 1999. Lou Bega, a German musician of Ugandan and Italian descent who was 24 years old at the time, released his rendition of "Mambo No. 5," which topped the Spanish, Austrian, Swiss, Dutch, and German music charts and sold 13 million copies while staying at number 1 for 10 straight weeks.

Martin, Lopez, and Bega were only three of the new Latin music artists who had broad demographic appeal. As choreographer Chitons Rivera said, "This is an amazing thing that's happening now. Everybody wants to live the la Veda local [life on the move]."

Low-Budget "Mockumentary" Becomes Most Profitable Film

In 1999 the low-budget independent movie *The Blair Witch Project* surprised critics and audiences when it became a cult phenomenon and then found box-office success. An innovative online advertising and promotion campaign helped the movie gross $140 million, which was way less than big-budget blockbusters like *Star Wars* and *Titanic*. However, the University of Central Florida film students who created the movie, Daniel Myrick and Eduardo Sanchez, only spent $30,000 to make it, so its net earnings made it the most profitable movie of all time.

The movie was shot in eight days with an evolving script that changed daily. It featured unknown actors and was shot entirely with handheld film and video cameras, which resulted in shaky images that made some moviegoers dizzy and nauseous, but this effect only enhanced the movie's mystique. The movie marketing took advantage of the late 1990s obsession with "reality programming," videotapes, and the Internet as millions of curious folks went to *The Blair Witch Project* website to "research" made-up details that were not in the movie. As one fan put it "Netizens have finally seen their own image on the big screen and are ready for more."

The Mir Space Station

The space station Mir was the result of Soviet efforts to maintain a human presence in space for the long haul. At least two cosmonauts inhabited Mir on a permanent basis, and they used the space station to perform ongoing technical and scientific experiments. By the decade's end, Mir had completed 79,300 trips around the Earth in 13 years of orbit while hosting the astronauts and cosmonauts from numerous nations.

In the 1990s NASA docked nine shuttles with Mir, and these missions helped create the International Space Station because Mir inspired the project. Furthermore, seven American astronauts spent time aboard Mir, including Shannon W. Lucid, who spent six months aboard the Russian space station, which earned her the title of America's most experienced astronaut.

On Planet Venus with Serena

In spite of her age at the end of 1999, 19-year-old Venus Williams had been on the tennis scene as a high-profile player for years. A 6'1", 167 pound-player with braided hair that incorporated 1,800 beads, she was hard to miss, on and off the court. For half of the 1990s, she was the topic of conversation in women's tennis, both for her level of play and her controversial father Richard, who was her first coach and current manager. Her father called her "ghetto Cinderella" because of her upbringing in a crime-riddled area of Los Angeles. She grew up playing tennis with "dead" balls on cracked neighborhood courts full of broken glass.

However, there is more; Venus had a younger sister who was even more dominating on the tennis court. Their forceful father had formulated a plan for the sisters from an early age. They first took to the court at age 4, and the hard work paid off. Before Venus played her first professional match, she had already amassed $12 million in endorsement contracts. She won her first professional title in 1998 at the age of 17.

When the decade ended, Venus had already won nine singles titles and claimed $2 million in prize money. Serena, on the other hand, caught up to her sister and then surpassed her to become the first of the siblings to win a Grand Slam title when they played at the U.S. Open in 1999. The two were even better when paired in doubles competitions, winning two Grand Slam doubles titles in 1999, the French Open and the U.S. Open.

Genetic Engineering and Dolly the Sheep

Many anxious observers feared the ethical implications of a new form of science and technology called genetic engineering. Their fears grew more worrisome when Ian Wilmut of the Roslin Institute in Scotland successfully cloned a sheep from the cell of an adult ewe. They worried that the science used to create the sheep named "Dolly" would one day be used to clone humans.

In 1993, four years before Dolly, researchers at George Washington University cloned human embryos in a Petri dish and nurtured them for several days. The project provoked protests from politicians and religious leaders, and when scientists created headless mice, people worried that the next step would be to create headless human clones to supply organs to their "parent." As a result, President Clinton banned human cloning in federally sponsored laboratories and asked private researchers to comply with the ban.

The Threat of Y2K

A huge concern during the last year of the decade was the "Y2K" bug. As early as 1997, technology experts determined that many computers might not recognize the year 2000 as valid. In other words, the machines would count from "99" to "00," and the result would mean the crashing of systems across the planet from everywhere from ATM machines to electrical grids. People even feared that hospital equipment would stop functioning and atomic weapons would autonomously detonate.

The phrase "Y2K ready" became commonplace on everything advertised from banks to national government agencies, which meant they had diagnosed and fixed the potential issue. For others, the Y2K situation signaled the end of the world, and more than ever before, people bought generators and stocked up on canned food, bottles of water, and guns and ammunition to prepare for the presumed chaos.

Fortunately, the world survived, and a new millennium full of brand new hope was born.

20 RANDOM FACTS FROM 1999

1. On January 25, 1999, 1,170 people died in Columbia following an earthquake measuring 6.3 on the Richter scale.

2. On February 7, 1999, King Hussein in Jordan died from cancer after 46 years in power. His son, King Abdullah, succeeded him.

3. On February 12, 1999, President Clinton was acquitted on both Articles of Impeachment.

4. On February 24, 1999, the 41st Grammy Awards awarded Album of the Year for *The Miseducation of Lauryn Hill* and Record of the Year for "My Heart Will Go On" by Celine Dion.

5. On March 1, 1999, an international treaty banning land mines went into effect. All signers of the treaty had to destroy their stockpiles of mines within 4 years and clear all mines on their territory within 10 years.

6. On March 21, 1999, the 71st Academy Awards awarded *Shakespeare in Love* as Best Picture, and Gwyneth Paltrow as Best Actress for her role in the movie. Robert Benigni won Best Actor for his role in *Life is Beautiful*.

7. On March 21, 1999, Swiss psychiatrist Bertrand Piccard and British pilot Brian Jones became the first men to fly around the world in a balloon.

Their balloon, Breitling Orbiter 3, landed in the Egyptian desert after a journey of 25,362 miles in 21 days.

8. On March 24, 1999, NATO Operation Allied Force began. The operation was a massive bombing campaign in the province of Kosovo against Yugoslav targets in order to protect the Albanian majority.

9. On March 26, 1999, the Melissa computer virus appeared, creating havoc on e-mail systems and infecting 19 percent of U.S. corporations. David L. Smith was arrested on April 2 for setting off the virus.

10. On March 29, 1999, the Dow Jones closed above 10,000 for the first time.

11. On April 12, 1999, President Clinton was held in contempt of civil court for giving false and misleading answers designed to obstruct justice when he was asked about his relationship with Monica Lewinsky. It was the first time in U.S. history that a president had obstructed the judicial process while serving. Clinton was required to pay the court $1,200.

12. On May 3, 1999, the Dow Jones closed above 11,000 for the first time, making the fastest 1,000-point gain in history.

13. On May 19, 1999, *Star Wars: Episode I: The Phantom Menace* was released, breaking a string of box office records and grossing $102.7 million in five days.

14. In May 1999 archeologists discovered a Mayan city in a dense forest on the Yucatan Peninsula in Mexico.

15. On June 6 the unemployment rate was 4.8 percent, the lowest it had been since 1973.

16. In June 1999 the computer virus Worm.Explore.Zip infiltrated systems around the nation through email, burrowing into software, erasing files, and shutting down networks, including Microsoft. Boeing's network was shut down for seven days.

17. On July 23-25, 1999, Woodstock '99 was held in Rome, New York. Concertgoers complained that the spirit of the original Woodstock was compromised and commercialized when crowds set fires and destroyed property during the closing act. Several sexual assaults and rapes were reported.

18. On August 17, 1999, Turkey was struck by its worst natural disaster in 60 years: a devastating earthquake that measured 7.4 on the Richter Scale that killed 17,000 people.

19. In 1999 *Forbes* declared the richest person in the world to be Bill Gates with a $36.4 billion net worth and reported him to be followed by the Walton family of Wal-Mart retailers at $27.6 billion and Warren Buffet at $25.2 billion.

20. In 1999 half of the world's population was aged under 25, with 95 percent of the growth occurring in the Third World.

TEST YOUR 1999 KNOWLEDGE
10 QUESTIONS

1) Which Latin music pop star from the 1990s said that he grew up listening to Journey, Foreigner, Cheap Trick, and Boston?

   a) Ricky Martin
   b) Jennifer Lopez
   c) Lou Bega

2) Which movie from 1999 became the most profitable film of all time?

   a) *Star Wars: Episode I: The Phantom Menace*
   b) *Titanic*
   c) *The Blair Witch Project*

3) Who won the 1999 U.S. Open in tennis?

   a) Serena Williams
   b) Venus Williams
   c) Martina Hingis

4) What was the name of the sheep that was cloned at the Roslin Institute in Scotland in the 1990s?

   a) Dolly
   b) Ewe
   c) Maximus

5) What technology glitch caused many people to fear the end of the decade?

   a) Y2K

b) Melissa computer virus
c) Worm.Explore.Zip

6) What was the result of Bill Clinton's impeachment hearings?

a) Clinton was acquitted of both accounts
b) He was held in contempt of court
c) All of the above

7) In 1999 the Dow Jones eclipsed what mark for the first time?

a) 4,000 points
b) 7,000 points
c) 11,000 points

8) What was the Breitling Orbiter 3, and what did it help two men do?

a) A balloon; fly around the world
b) A plane; fly around the world without refueling
c) A boat; break the record for fastest time across the Atlantic

9) In 1999 Gwyneth Paltrow won an Academy Award for her role in what film?

a) *Shakespeare in Love*
b) *Life is Beautiful*
c) *Se7en*

10) In 1999 what did archeologists discover in the dense forest of the Yucatan Peninsula?

a) Mayan calendar
b) Mayan city
c) The remains of the fifth Aztec emperor, Montezuma I

ANSWERS

1) a
2) c
3) a
4) a
5) a
6) c
7) c
8) a
9) a
10) b

More Books by Bill O'Neill

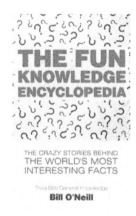

THE CRAZY STORIES BEHIND
THE WORLD'S MOST
INTERESTING FACTS

Trivia Bits General Knowledge
Bill O'Neill

Have you ever wondered what happens to luggage that goes unclaimed at the airport? How about the origin of naming hurricanes after people? For a behind-the-scenes look at some of the craziest, interesting, and need-to-know facts, we've got you covered with The Fun Knowledge Encyclopedia: The Crazy Stories Behind the World's Most Interesting Facts. The book contains hundreds of trivia facts and stories, ranging from the interesting and informative to the simply outrageous.

Are you the trivia buff in your friend group? Maybe you're just always hoping to learn more random facts to keep up your sleeve. Whether you're a regular trivia fanatic or someone looking for a fun read, the book goes beyond the scope of general knowledge into some of the most interesting facts and intriguing trivia tidbits out there.

Everyone can use some fun facts in their life! No other fact books cover anything and everything from the most insane rent agreement in New York history, to the way in which the Titanic disaster could potentially have been averted. The knowledge encyclopedia you've been searching for is finally here.

Learn how much a hot dog cart permit costs in New York City, and explore some of the oddest houses in the world. The Fun Knowledge Encyclopedia: The Crazy Stories Behind the World's Most Interesting Facts is the trivia book of all trivia books. Find everything you've ever wanted-- but never quite needed-- to know, all under one cover.

DON'T FORGET YOUR FREE BOOKS

**GET THEM FOR FREE ON
WWW.TRIVIABILL.COM**

MORE BOOKS BY BILL O'NEILL

I hope you enjoyed this book and learned something new. Please feel free to check out some of my previous books on Amazon.